Here is a collection of some of the funniest pieces ever written by Dan Rattiner. Serious, witty, nonsensical, gauch and completely unique, Rattiner has earned a place in New York literary circles as the East Coast's finest satirist and humorist.

In this volume are such famous pieces as "The Reindeer Who Couldn't Fly" (a fairytale), "The Hampton Light and Power Co.", "Cecil Pontopolis and the Six Million Dollar Parking Ticket" and over 35 more hilarious moments of truth on the morals and foibles of the human species.

Albert Einstein's Summer Vacation

and other stories

by
Dan Rattiner
illustrated by the author

Published by Publishing Tower Press
Bridgehampton, N.Y. 11932

ALBERT EINSTEIN'S
SUMMER VACATION
© 1980 by Publishing Tower Press

Chapters in this book previously appeared as stories and articles in Dan's Papers during the years 1974, 1975, 1976, 1977, 1978 or 1979.
Typeset in 10 Point Mallard Book Face.

ISBN: 0-9604018-0-6

Library of Congress Catalog Number: 80-80336

Printed in the United States of America

Contents

For Tracy.

Albert Einstein's Summer Vacation

On a still, warm morning in June, 1939, a handsome woman walked into Rothman's Department Store on the Main Street of Southold and began looking at items on the shelves.

David Rothman, 42, sucked on his pipe.

There is something about her, he thought. She looks very familiar.

Rothman had been standing by the cash register in the back of the store, listening to a recording of Handel's Water Music, and now he turned the volume down and walked toward the front door.

"May I help you?"

"Yes. I don't suppose you would have such a thing, but I'm looking for a tool that is used to sharpen a sculptor's chisel."

"Hm," Rothman said. He thought for a moment. "As a matter of fact, I think I DO have such a thing. It's been around for a long time. Nobody's bought it, of course. But I'll bet I know just where it is."

Rothman disappeared behind a glass showcase and began to rummage around on a shelf high up on a wall. There were toys, clothes, games, pots and pans, jackets, all the sorts of things you might expect in an old-fashioned general merchandise store.

"Ah, here we are," Rothman said.

He brought the device down.

"I beg your pardon," he said, "but you look awfully familiar to me. Have you been in my store before?"

"No. As a matter of fact, we're new in town. My father and I have rented a place for the summer on Nassau Point."

"You're Margot," Rothman said.

"Yes. How did you know?"

"I recognize you from your picture. You're Margot Wibtelar, and your father is Albert Einstein. I've read everything he's ever written. Everything about him. I've seen your picture in magazines."

"My goodness."

"Please take this sharpener with my compliments. And give my regards to your illustrious father."

"Oh, I couldn't."

"Yes, you could. It is a privilege to have Albert Einstein in our town."

*   *   *

What was relativity all about? How did this incredible discovery, which Rothman had read so avidly about in his department store in Southold, relate the microcosm to the macrocosm? What was the great man working on now? The following morning, as Rothman opened Rothman's Department Store for another day, he hardly dared think that the great Albert Einstein was in their midst for the summer. Perhaps he could arrange some way to get a glimpse of this great man.

And then, at eleven A.M., Albert Einstein appeared at the front door of Rothman's Department Store. He was unmistakable. With a great shock of white hair (Einstein was 60 at the time), a broad midriff and white boxer shorts and sandals, there was never the slightest question that this was he. Rothman's heart was pounding in his chest.

Einstein shuffled in.

I must treat him like any other customer, Rothman thought.

"May I help you?"

"Yes," Einstein said. "My daughter told me one could find anything one wanted in your store. I am looking for sundials."

"Sundials, sundials," Rothman said. "Let me look."

Rothman looked everywhere in the store. Under boxes. On top of shelves. But there were no sundials.

"I thought surely there were some," he finally said. "But you know, I do have one of my own out in the yard out back. Come with me. If you like it you can have it. If not, I can always order for you what you want."

Einstein looked puzzled, but did as he was told and followed David Rothman through the piles of merchandise, past the record player which was issuing forth Mozart's G Minor Symphony, and out the back door into the yard. There stood a beautiful cement sundial, about three feet high.

"No, no," Einstein said. He lifted a leg and touched his foot with his hand. "Sundials. Sundials."

Oh, my God, Rothman thought. He's wearing sandals.

"Them I got!" he shouted. And they went back inside.

*   *   *

The sandals cost one dollar and fifty cents, and as Rothman was putting them into a bag, he noticed that Albert Einstein was unconsciously conducting the Mozart Symphony with his hands.

"I see you like music," Rothman ventured.

"Oh, yes, I am an amateur violinist."

"Well, that's a coincidence. So am I. My name is David Rothman." Rothman extended his hand.

"Mr. Rothman. I'm Albert Einstein. We must play together then some evening."

"Oh, I don't want to interfere with your vacation," Rothman said. "It's up to you."

Einstein took the package and tucked it under his arm.

11

"Monday night will be a good night," he said as he walked out the door. "Bring some sheet music."

*   *   *

What sort of sheet music does one take to a concert with Albert Einstein? Easy pieces? Hard pieces? Certainly one doesn't want to show up the great man in any way. Perhaps it would be the best thing to take a little of everything.

Rothman took a wide variety of sheet music from his library, his violin and case, and his music stand, said goodbye to his wife Ruth, and walked out the door to his Durant Sedan. Slowly, nervously, he drove it through Southold, down Nassau Point Road, and out toward the Einstein summer house on Old Cove Road. When he arrived, he was greeted at the door by Einstein's personal secretary, Miss Ducas, and led across a porch and into the living room where the scientist was waiting.

"Let me take your things," Einstein said. "Sit down, make yourself comfortable. Did you bring some music? Something easy? Something more difficult?"

The two men chatted for a bit, and then Einstein went through the sheet music and chose Bach's Double Concerto. It was, Rothman knew, one of the very difficult pieces. And in a very short time, perhaps just a few bars, Rothman knew that he was out of his league. Einstein played his half of the

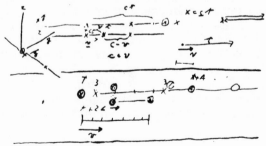

piece with ease, while Rothman struggled with his. After a brief fashion, they stopped in the middle.

"Let's put the music down for now," Einstein said. "Let's go out on the porch and talk."

Thus ended, almost as soon as it started, the first musicale between Einstein and Rothman. It was eight o'clock in the evening. What was to follow was beyond Rothman's wildest imaginations.

"Where did you learn to play?" Einstein asked as they settled into wicker chairs on the porch.

"I'm self taught," Rothman said. "But we have a quartet at my house every week, so I try to keep up."

"I'm largely self taught, too," Einstein said. "I learned in Germany."

"You have just come out?"

"I fled the Nazis two years ago. I've just recently come to America. So you'll have to pardon my English."

"I have been reading about almost everything you have done," Rothman said. "And I have so many questions to ask you. What are you working on now?"

"A unified field theory. I am working out a relationship between the macrocosm and the microcosm."

"That seems fairly simple," Rothman said. "The planets revolve around the sun. The electrons revolve around the nucleus. Clearly there is a relationship."

Einstein lit a pipe. "It's actually rather difficult," he said. "I'm not interested so much in the particles as I am the spaces between them."

"Oh."

"And when I get it done, I'm not sure I'll be able to prove the theory. Tell me. You seem so curious about everything, Mr. Rothman, and here you are a dry goods merchant. Are you an educated man?"

"I am self educated," Rothman said. "I was never very interested in school and the current events they teach. So I studied myself. Plato. Newton. Bacon."

"I wasn't much interested in school either," Einstein said.

The two men sat on that porch that evening talking for four more hours, about every subject, about every great book. Somehow, in that single evening, a rapport was established between the great scientist and the dry goods merchant.

At midnight, Miss Ducas appeared in the doorway in her nightgown.

"You are keeping the doctor up so late," she said.

"But I am keeping Mr. Rothman up late," Einstein said.

Einstein asked if he could join the quartet that Rothman had mentioned earlier in the evening, and Rothman replied that surely he could. They would be having a musicale just a few days later in the week.

Miss Ducas gathered up Rothman's things and ushered him to the door. As she and Einstein said goodbye, she leaned forward and whispered, "This quartet, Mr. Rothman, it must not be jazz players."

And then Rothman was out the door.

* * *

Thus began a strong and close friendship between Albert Einstein and David Rothman. In the days that followed, Rothman and Einstein took hikes together, went on outings together. Einstein had a tiny sailboat, not much larger than a rowboat — he called it "Tinif," which is Yiddish for "Junk" — and he sailed this little boat on Peconic Bay wearing an undershirt, baggy shorts and a folded-up newspaper hat on his head to keep his white hair from blowing.

Einstein also asked his neighbor if he couldn't have permission to use a path alongside the neighbor's yard as a shortcut to the beach. But the neighbor refused.

"We are here for our privacy, just as you, Mr. Einstein," the neighbor said.

Twice a week, Einstein would come to the Rothman household to play in the evening quartets there. Attending these quartets were Rothman's brother-in-law, Milton Samuel, a viola player; Howard Cook, a cellist; and Robert Lyon, also a cellist. Oddly, at this time, Rothman had taken in for the summer a melancholy, 26-year-old composer named Benjamin Britten. Occasionally, Britten would play in the quartets, but for the most part Britten spent his time upstairs building model airplanes with Rothman's son. Britten made almost no contact with Einstein, though he was to go on to be the most famous contemporary composer of the age. At that time he was simply a confused young man, a British subject who refused to join the war, who had fled London and found himself on eastern Long Island.

In fact, one day Britten asked if he couldn't take a job as a clerk in the Rothman Department Store. Perhaps this was his calling. Rothman refused and told him to stick to composing.

*   *   *

Einstein and Rothman often walked on the beach together. Once they went out at night by flashlight.

"If I take this flashlight beam and shine it up," Rothman said, "then it would travel forever. Is that true?"

"If it gets through the atmosphere."

"Do you believe in God?" Rothman asked.

There was a long silence.

"I do not believe in an anthropomorphic God," Einstein said. "You know this word 'anthropomorphic'?"

"Yes."

"For me, religion takes the form of a rapturous amazement at the harmony and beauty and mathematical preciseness that obtains in the Universe. It reveals an intelligence of such superiority that human intelligence is totally insignificant before it. I'm filled with wonder, awe and humbleness."

Rothman memorized this, almost word for word, Later, he was talking alone to Einstein's secretary, Miss Ducas.

"Miss Ducas, you should be taking notes," Rothman said. "If we only had notes about Newton, about Gallileo, it would be so wonderful to read them now."

"Don't worry," Miss Ducas said. "I'm taking them."

*   *   *

A week later, Rothman thought to take Einstein on an outing to the Riverhead Telegraph Receiving Station. This was a major station that could receive messages from all over Europe, and Rothman had a lot of friends at the station. He thought Einstein would enjoy meeting them and seeing the place.

The two of them started out, driving slowly in Rothman's sedan and they had gotten as far as Peconic when another car cut them off and pulled them over. Rothman recognized the driver who was getting out of his car as a salesman from the Allen Card Company.

"Hi, Mr. Rothman. Gee, is that EinSTEEN?"

"Yes, it is, Andy."

"Sorry to pull you over like this. But I stopped in your store and they told me you had just left and if I hurried I could catch you. I won't be back out this way for another two weeks. You need anything?"

"Andy, I don't need a thing. Stop and see me next time."

"Okay, Mr. Rothman. And sorry again."

And the young salesman drove off.

"Gee," Rothman said to Einstein, "I hope this didn't frighten you, his pulling us off the road like that."

"No," Einstein said. "In Germany maybe this would have frightened me, but not here."

"You must have had a real tough time in Germany."

"Well, the Storm Troopers came to my house one night and they took my wife and me outside into the yard. They had to search my house for weapons they said, and so they went inside and out they came with my carving knives. 'See, we have found weapons,' they said. And they smashed my sailboat. I said to my wife, 'Look good on this place for you shall not see it again.' And that night my friends, they took us off to Holland and then to England." Einstein turned to Rothman. "And you know," he said, "if they had catched me, they would have killed me. Of that I am sure."

*   *   *

At this time, the Riverside Church in Manhattan had sent out letters to fifty scientists across the country. Their plan, they said, was to erect statues at the church to the eight most famous scientists that ever lived. Could the fifty scientists send in their lists of eight? They would like to know of whom these statues should be made.

The lists came in. And on every list there was only one name of a scientist still alive at the time: Albert Einstein. The statues were erected.

"How does it feel to have your statue there among Moses, Newton, Christ?" Rothman wanted to know.

"From now on," Einstein said, "and for the rest of my life, I must be very careful not to commit a scandal."

17

Einstein would often show up at Rothman's house unannounced. He would come in the back door, play with Rothman's children, lie down on the couch and take a snooze.

"Where is Ruth?" Einstein asked one day.

"My wife is in the hospital. She is quite sick and I've just come back."

"She'll be all right?"

"I think so. She is such a wonderful woman. I am so in love with her. I don't know what I would do without her."

"You know, I've had two wives," Einstein said, "but I have never experienced the love that you have. My wives have been good women who've looked after me."

In a few weeks, Ruth Rothman had fully recovered.

*   *   *

"Rothman. You want me to teach you the theory of relativity?"

"What? Are you kidding? With my eighth grade education?"

"If you had a college education, I'd be suspicious. With an eighth grade education, I think I can do it."

"What do you want me to do?"

"I need you to do a few things. Promise me you'll give me three full hours of your time. And promise me, if you get lost with what I say, you'll tell me. That way I could clarify things and we won't get all tangled up. Okay?"

"I need a promise from you."

"What's that?"

"That you won't use any mathematics. You've got to do the whole explanation without mathemetics."

"Agreed."

Einstein took out a pad and a pencil.

"I said no mathematics," Rothman said.

"I'm just going to take notes while I talk. You don't

mind if I do that."

"No, of course not."

Einstein began his discourse, talking about how a metal rod contracts in the direction of its spin. As he talked, Einstein wrote numbers and formulas on the paper he had in front of him. And then, forgetting himself, he lapsed into a complicated mathematical formula.

"We said no mathematics," Rothman said.

"But this was so TRIVIAL!" Einstein said.

And so, they gave up the effort. Rothman did, however, ask if he could keep the piece of paper on which Einstein was scribbling, which Einstein gladly gave him. A copy of this paper is reproduced on page 12.

* * *

On one occasion, Einstein, wearing his newspaper hat, undershirt and baggy shorts, was hauling his anchor in the middle of Peconic Bay when his boat capsized, Einstein was thrown into the water, and, since he could not swim, began thrashing around yelling for help. A 15-year-old boy who was swimming near by and who never identified himself, saved Einstein.

"I made a triple error," Einstein later told Rothman in his broken English.

On another occasion, Rothman got a phone call from Miss Ducas to inform him that Albert Einstein had decided to sail his little boat from Nassau Point to Rothman's house in Southold.

"He left at six a.m.," Miss Ducas said. "So he should be there soon."

But Einstein did not arrive. After the sun set, Rothman became hysterical that his friend had been lost. But then the phone rang. On the other end was a friend of Rothman's, a vacationing New York cop who lived at the Southold beach.

"Rothman. There's a weird looking guy who needs

a haircut — some helluva looking looney — down here on the beach wanting to know where you live."

Rothman sighed, and went to the rescue.

*　　*　　*

"Hello, Mr. Rothman? This is the minister from the Southold church, and the reason that I'm calling is that I understand you're a good friend of Einstein. Next week, I'm moderating a meeting at the Firehouse about getting refugees out of Nazi Germany. I know Mr. Einstein has been active in getting Jewish refugees out. We're going to try to get some of the Christian refugees out. What I wondered was, could you ask Mr. Einstein to attend? Just his presence there would be a big boost to us. You come too."

"Well, I'll ask him, and he'll probably say yes. But let me just warn you to please treat him like an ordinary person. Don't ask him to speak or anything. You might just mention that he's in the audience."

"Of course."

The following week, Rothman, wearing a suit and a tie, drove over to pick up Einstein on Nassau Point. Einstein came down to meet him wearing an undershirt, baggy pants tied up with a rope and sandals.

"My. You are looking elegant," Einstein said, looking over Rothman's suit. And he disappeared back upstairs. Ten minutes later he was back, dressed in more proper attire.

The meeting was attended by perhaps two hundred residents of Southold who all sat on folding chairs facing a dais. Einstein and Rothman were about halfway back.

"And we have with us," the minister said, "the famous scientist Albert Einstein. Mr. Einstein, come up to the dais and join us and give a little speech."

Einstein gave Rothman a funny look, then went up and sat. One speech followed another, and finally

Einstein was asked to say something.

"You must organize just as we Jews have organized," he said. "Otherwise you will have a big problem." Then he sat down. There was silence. That was it? Everyone applauded.

After the meeting broke up, literally dozens of people crowded around Rothman and Einstein trying to say a few words to them.

"Mr. Einstein," one woman said. "I'm from Europe. I understand you've come from Europe too?"

"Yes, Europe, a fine place," Einstein said. Then he turned to Rothman and cupped a hand over his mouth. "Get me out of here," he whispered.

Rothman led Einstein through the crowd and out onto the street where they began to walk toward Rothman's car. From behind a tree there jumped an older man who identified himself as a famous physicist from Johns Hopkins University. He just wanted to meet Albert Einstein he said, and so they shook hands and exchanged a few pleasantries.

A week later, this Johns Hopkins' physicist was at the counter in the Rothman Department Store.

"Mr. Rothman, you've got to lend me a hundred dollars."

"A hundred dollars? Why?"

"I've just been at the carnival down at the corner and there's a fellow running a cups and shells game and I've lost all my money. If you lend me a hundred dollars I'll win it back."

Rothman refused and, instead, called the police who took care of the matter. Later, he related the story to Einstein, reminding him that he'd met this professor outside the fire hall.

"We scientists are not good businessmen," Einstein said. "If we are good businessmen, we are not good scientists."

*   *   *

On the morning of July 30, 1939, an old Plymouth arrived at Einstein's vacation house bearing two scientists from Princeton University. Rothman was there at the time, and Einstein introduced them as Leo Szilard and Eugene P. Wigner. Rothman, seeing that they were there on serious business, excused himself and went back to Southold. He never did learn that Szilard and Wigner, together with Einstein who had greeted them in undershirt, rolled up pants and sandals, would proceed to draft one of the most famous letters of the Second World War. Addressed and sent to Franklin D. Roosevelt, it outlined the discoveries made by the Germans in developing an Atomic Bomb, and a plea for the creation of a program to create an atomic weapon that could alter the course of the war.

"A single bomb of this type," the letter said, "might very well destroy a whole port together with some of the surrounding territory."

Szilard and Wigner helped Einstein in drafting this letter but only Einstein signed it. Szilard and Wigner believed, correctly, that only a scientist of Einstein's stature could carry the weight necessary to see to it that the letter arrived on the President's desk.

The letter was mailed from Nassau Point on August 2, 1939 and reached the President on October 11. President Roosevelt ordered the creation of an atomic bomb study group as a result.

* * *

Einstein left Nassau Point in the autumn of 1939 to take up his position once again in Princeton, New Jersey. He did not return to Nassau Point the following summer, but instead wrote to Rothman and asked if his sailboat could be trucked to Saranac Lake in the Mountains. For family health reasons, he wrote, he would not be able to return to the beach, for which he was deeply grieved.

A lively correspondence was kept up between Einstein and Rothman over the next five years. When the government was trying to raise money for the war effort, they asked Einstein, now in Princeton, if he would write down, in his own hand, his theory of relativity, so they could raffle it off. This Einstein did, and in the raffle, a total of $6,000,000 was raised. Rothman wrote Einstein and reminded him of the piece of paper that he, Rothman, still had.

"And what became of your original manuscript on relativity?" Rothman wrote. "Did the Nazis get it?"

"My first manuscript was not burned by the Nazis," Einstein replied. "I myself threw it into the wastebasket after it was printed, judging it good for nothing."

A year later, the Einstein Unified Theory was published. It appeared as a front page story in the New York Times, and the Times quoted scientists who said that it was unlikely that this theory could either be proven or disproven in this generation.

Every year, Rothman sent Einstein a new pair of sandals.

"I miss the nights with your quartet group," Einstein wrote back. And then, in a later letter, he wrote, "I am thinking often of the beautiful hours we spent together in the last years. . ."

In 1946, Einstein and Rothman met for the last time. They embraced, and Einstein said, "I have had the most wonderful summers of my entire life and this I owe to your initiative."

The account of Einstein's visit to the North Fork was obtained through a lengthy interview with David Rothman. Mr. Rothman, now in his eighties, still runs the Rothman's Department Store in Southold, though he is largely retired. The day we were there [we bought toys for the children, flashlight batteries, and a Havahart mousetrap], the store was being manned by David's son Bob and grandson Ron. Ron Rothman, who is in his twenties, befriended this author two years ago, and has attended folk song musicales at this author's home monthly over those past two years. Such are the coincidences of life.

A few more words should be said about Einstein's visit to the North Fork in 1939. At that time, it had already been twenty-five years since Einstein had advanced the Theory of Relativity. It was also fifteen years since that theory had been proven by scientific demonstration. At this time in 1939, Einstein was already deeply in thought about his Unified Field Theory. He conjectured, back in the 1920's, that since he had been able to develop a Unified Force Theory [the Relativity Theory], then there should also be a corresponding Unified Field Theory.

Unfortunately, during the decades that Einstein was working on his Field Theory, other scientists advanced the Quantum Theory which explained the Field situation in a way quite different than Einstein proposed. Thus, for the entire last half of his life Einstein worked as a maverick, totally cut out of the mainstream of the scientists who embraced the Quantum Theory. By 1939, Einstein, though respected for his earlier work, was largely isolated by the scientific community. "It is a shame that such a brilliant man could waste the last half of his life in such a way," one of his students said.

But was it wasted? It will take the minds of future generations to either prove or disprove Einstein's Unified Field Theory. We must wait and see.

Artist-Writers Game

Every summer, a baseball game is held on the baseball diamond behind the A&P in East Hampton between the "artists" and the "writers." This may seem like some sort of a joke, but actually there are so many well-known artists in the Hamptons, and so many well-known writers, that this game is usually a good place to go to view celebrities. In the past few years, it has been possible to watch a number of very famous people strike out or bumble balls around the infield, trying to do something they have never been trained to do. Coming to mind are such "writers" and "artists" as Woody Allen, Abbie Hoffman, Gwen Verdon and Dustin Hoffman. I have this wonderful memory of Abbie Hoffman successfully stealing second base.

One of the most puzzling aspects of the Writers'-Artists' game, and the game is always held for charity, is that the writers always win. I mean, this would not be unusual if the game had only been held three times with three victories for the writers, but the game has taken place since 1968, and since that time, the results have been as follows:

1968 Writers 20 Artists 2
1969 Writers 16 Artists 2
1970 Writers 8 Artists 6
1971 Writers 11 Artists 6
1972 Writers 7 Artists 5
1973 Writers 13 Artists 12

I think you can see this is a very disturbing

situation. In all these years, with some of the greatest minds in the country participating in or watching
the annual game, nobody has ever been able to come
up with an adequate explanation for the writers'
unusual superiority in this sport.

This year's baseball game was held on the Sunday
of Labor Day weekend, a sunny day but a chilly one,
with the first hint of the autumn weather already in
the air. There were about three or four hundred
people on hand to watch this game — a small crowd
by usual standards — and some people attributed it
to the fact that it was already the end of the
summer, that the starch was out of it, and the people
already had their minds elsewhere, namely on the
melancholy trip back to the City. I don't know. That
could be the case.

Anyway, the scene consisted of a sandlot baseball
field with a hurricane fence backstop, ten rows of
wooden stands behind home plate, a bunch of
swings and seesaws for the children, and an outfield
that goes off and merges into a football field in one
dirction and a tennis court in the other. There is a
large maple tree on the foul side of the first base
line, but if you hit a fly ball in the air over first base,
you'll undoubtedly hit a limb. Also, on the foul side
of the third base line, off in left field, is the
paved-over and fenced-in parking lot of the A&P.
Towering foul balls on the left side invariably fall in
this lot, necessitating a considerable wait for the
ball.

It was into these homey and rather pleasant
circumstances that I arrived for the game about five
minutes before game time. Now, in previous years, I
have been used as something of a reserve for the
writers' team. I am hardly a famous writer,
although I could be considered an aspiring one.

Furthermore, I hardly ever play baseball anymore, considering it a lot if I might swing a bat twice in the course of a year. My fielding is legendary for its absence, and when I am put in as a substitute late in the game, I generally manage to get myself located at second base, a position that rarely gets any action, and which is safely hidden behind the towering form of the pitcher. It is from this vantage point that I can usually watch in peace while the writers complete the annual trounce of the artists.

I should have known that something was amiss when I went up to the man in charge of the writers (one hates to call him or anyone else a manager of this fracas), Willie Morris.

"You are starting," Willie said. "You're playing third base."

"Third base? That's the hottest position in the entire game!"

"That's right."

"I can't play third base. Let me play second base."

"We already have someone on second base."

"But I'll drop everything if I play third base. Get somebody else."

Willie Morris looked me up and down.

"Give it a try," he said.

It occurred to me briefly that Willie Morris might have thought of me as a young ringer, a wiry super-athlete put in to handle the hot corner of third base. But that couldn't possibly be the case. I am now thirty-five, my hair is greying, and I move with the grace of, say, what shall I say? Be kind. No. There had to be another reason I was being asked to play third base, and I thought I knew what it was. After six years, the writers were going to be giving the artists a chance. I was merely a pawn in the greater scheme of things.

Now here is a story I fully intend to tell my grandchildren.

After my anguishing conversation with Willie Morris, I looked over toward third base and saw our starting first baseman bending over to tie his sneaker, pending the start of the game. He was Eugene McCarthy, the man who had run for President of the United States in 1968, and who now wore rumpled pants with a little split in the back that widened when he bent over.

"Mr. McCarthy," I said, trotting over. "I'm your third baseman. I haven't thrown a baseball from third to first in eight years. When we get out in the field, I'd appreciate it if you could throw me a few ground balls so I could throw the ball from third to first."

For the benefit of those unfamiliar with the game of baseball, I should say that the hard part of playing third base is being hit very hard and very frequent ground balls, and then having to throw them accurately across the field to first base. I was now suggesting to the Presidential Candidate that we might practice this exercise a little bit.

"Right," Mr. McCarthy said.

On first base, he tossed me a few slow ground balls through the infield grass, and I threw them accurately to him at first. He then threw me one I had to run a little bit for, and, overconfident, I grabbed it, made a complete 350 degree turn, and threw the ball twenty feet straight up. It made a graceful arc and came down on the head of a man who had just sold a Jackson Pollack to an Australian museum for two million dollars. Ben Heller rubbed his head. Eugene McCarthy scowled at me. Pitcher

George Plimpton scowled at me. Peter Maas, author of "Serpico," frowned at me from second base. I smiled wanly. That's the story.

The game began, and it quickly became apparent that I was correct in my second observation. I was a weak link at third base. I booted a ground ball, and there were runners on first and second. Another ball was hit to shortstop, and I ran to third base to try and stop the art director of New York Magazine who was coming in standing up. But the throw to me was wild, and he went in to score. There were other people out there, also pawns in the greater scheme of things. By the end of the second inning, the writers were behind by four to nothing, and looking like they might get a lot worse.

"We've got to start spring training earlier next year," Willie Morris kept saying, referring to the fact that most of the players had just met about twenty minutes earlier.

One bright spot in the batting for the writers team, though, turned out to be Eugene McCarthy. Here he was, a man of about fifty, with iron-grey hair and distinquished features. A former Senator from Minnesota, he was now an editor for a New York publishing firm. He'd stand there at the plate, wiggling the bat and wherever that first pitch was, he'd smack it far into the air down the left field line. His first time at bat, he hit a scorching double, and his second time up, in the third inning, he scored the writers' only run.

On that occasion, he hit five towering foul balls down the third base line in a row before connecting one fair.

"Gene is aiming a little more to the left than he usually does," the announcer said over the loud speaker.

In the fifth inning, Gene McCarthy hit another single, and then was taken out for a pinch runner on first base. Keeping in mind there has been much debate about whether McCarthy will be a candidate in 1976, the announcer came up with another gem.

"McCarthy won't run," he shouted gleefully as Gene was led away.

If they elected presidents on their batting ability, there would be no doubt about Gene McCarthy. Now that's not such a bad criteria, is it?

The game wore on, and the writers, indeed, got worse. By the time it ended, with the sun low in the sky behind right field, the writers were behind by ten to one. During the last of that inning, a man in tennis clothes wandered across the left field lawn, a position I had been delegated to by this time.

"Who is winning," he smiled.

"The artists, ten to one."

He stopped as if struck by lightning. "NO!" he said.

After the game was over, and before everyone had adjourned to MOON Restaurant for a free beer party, there was considerable speculation about the collapse of the writers as a baseball team. Through it all, I kept thinking it was really Watergate that did it. The writers had burned themselves out, scribbling and typing away through the long months of the Watergate scandal. And what had the artists done through all this time? Nothing, that's what. While the writers were on the front line, the artists were back there in the woods in their studios, painting leisurely away, stretching canvas, mixing paint, ignoring the problems of the world, and drinking Gatorade. They were as lean as hounds' teeth when the big game came. And no doubt about it, they got their revenge.

Life With a Digital Clock

The shaft of morning light came to rest on a single bloodshot eye at the edge of the covers.

Oh, my God, the owner of the bloodshot eye intoned. Morning. What a party.

Fingers protruded from the covers, grasped it and pulled it up to block the shaft of morning light. Now there was just a wild mop of brown, oily hair at the edge of the covers.

The digital clock glowed.

Seven O Seven. God. Seven O Seven. Landing in San Juan. Then to the Dorado Beach Hotel. Terrible sunburn. Twisted ankle playing tennis. Maria. Beautiful Maria, of the black eyes and the shining hair. Alone with her in a hammock on the beach, swinging back and forth, asleep, fast asleep. . .

Seven Eleven. Orange juice. On the way home from the party I was supposed to stop at the Seven Eleven and pick up some milk, and some orange juice for Kathy. How did I get home from the party anyway? Where is Kathy? What happened after that girl took off her shirt? Maybe I'll just. . .

Seven Twenty-One. Firestone. The tire going bald. That cop stopped Anne and me and he was going to give me a ticket about it. Got to get a Seven Twenty-One today. I think they're Seven Twenty-Ones. I think anyway. . .

Seven Twenty-Seven. Screeching to a halt on the runway at Truman Airport in St. Thomas. God, that is a short runway down there, scaring the beejeezus out of everybody. When are they going to lengthen that runway anyhow? Seems I remember reading about that Seven Twenty-Seven that plowed into the gas station there at the end of the runway. I remember that gas station. A hot night. Stopped there in a yellow Volks Convertible with Jeanette on our way to the Palm Cafe. Steel band music. . .

Seven Forty-Seven. Oh yes, that wonderful inflight movie on the way to Europe, all curled up with Agnes. Earpieces in the way. Luggage in the way. Blankets and winter coats thrown all over with that young minister and his wife in the next seat. Skiers. Bound for Geneva and Mt. Blanc. Just a way to get that much closer to God, they said. . .

A snuffling and licking tickled an ear. Paws poking at the form under the blanket. Damn dog has to go out. Better get up.

How the Sun Will Burn Out

In reading a book on astronomy recently, I learned what scientists expect for the future of our sun. What they expect is that the sun will continue to shine, relatively unchanged for the next five billion years. During that time, it will burn up the hydrogen located in the core of the sun, and then it will begin to consume some of the hydrogen in the outer regions. When this happens, five billion years from now, the sun will begin to swell into a larger star, becoming what is known in astronomer's language as a "red giant." This will go on for another five billion years during which time, as the sun enlarges, it will consume the three closest planets in the solar system: Mercury, Venus and Earth. Finally, however, the sun will use up all the hydrogen in its outer regions and, when that happens, it will begin to burn out and slowly collapse. After another billion years or so, it will contract into a small star which will be called a "white dwarf" and then, through a process still not completely understood, it will shrink even smaller and smaller, becoming denser and denser, with an ever increasing pull of gravity until it finally disappears entirely into something called a "black hole."

The most interesting part of all this — well, the most disturbing anyway — was the part where the sun swells up and consumes Mercury, Venus and Earth. Personally, I have a lot at stake in this projected holocaust. In the attic, for example, I have all the notebooks from all the courses I took in college. I also have all the back issues of my newspapers dating back to 1960, filled with much of the material I have written, plus several books of poetry, handwritten, which have never been published, but which I am counting on being discovered by future generations of literary critics.

In the garage there is a rubber boat, all folded up, that I used for three months in Guatemala in the winter of 1969, and which future historians might find of considerable value. There is a 1961 Lambretta motorscooter with a broken camshaft that I used when I lived up in Boston, and there is a plaque that I received, fully engraved, for winning second place in the South Mountain New Jersey Grammar School Conservation Essay Contest in 1948.

The prospect of all this stuff, not to say all the future stuff that I might accumulate over the next few years, going up in some great solar bonfire is about as depressing a thought as I've had all morning.

On the other hand, the whole problem does not seem to be one that will become serious for at least eight or nine billion years. Furthermore, there are some great minds at work, with far more to lose in the holocaust than I, who will surely be working on some solutions. For instance, could it be possible to tie some jet engines to the earth and, as the sun expands, slowly propel the Earth a bit out in the direction of Mars so it is safely out of the way?

Or, might it be possible, at the last minute, to sort of pack everything up and move it to another planet, in the same way that people clear out the possessions of a condemned house before a road comes through and they have to knock the place down?

I thought about this, but I really could not imagine people combing through my college notebooks and old possessions, working feverishly to get everything into cardboard boxes before the holocaust comes.

Maybe I just ought to have a yard sale.

Wayne Miller and The Bootleg Hooch

The only day that Wayne Miller ever got in trouble was Friday, August 24. The day was clear and sunny and it started ordinarily enough. Wayne had climbed out of bed at the first morning light. He had pulled on his shirt, pants and boots as quietly as possible so as not to wake his snoring wife. He stuck on his cap. And then he had walked down the dusty road that served as Montauk's Main Street in 1927 to his lobster boat, the MARY ANNE. First, though, he stopped for a cup of coffee at Sheila's Harborside Cafe. The place was filled with fishermen's cigarette smoke and noise, as it always was at that hour.

"Heard they wuz all over town last night," a fellow fisherman said as Wayne slid onto a stool at the counter.

"Oh yeah?"

"A couple of big limousines. People runnin' all around. Must have been payday." The man turned the page of the magazine he was reading over his coffee.

"Naw, I slept through the whole thing. I'm a heavy sleeper."

Sheila slipped a mug in front of Wayne.

"You should have been here about an hour ago," she said. "Three of them stopped in with their shiny suits. Paid for everything in silver dollars."

"Must have been the end of their day," Wayne said.

"Sure is a lot of money in rumrunning," the other fisherman said. "Hey now, look here at this new Ford automobile." The man tapped the magazine.

"This convertible here is just like the one I saw one of these men drivin' the other night. Brand NEW."

Wayne stirred his coffee in silence. Through the open window he could see a dozen fishermen in rough clothes, readying their boats for the day's fishing. There was Pierre from Cape Breton. There was Frank who dragged for fish with his brothers, Ed and Jimmie. There was Frenchy, a man who worked with his wife, and who had also come down from Cape Breton. And there were many others.

To a man — and to a woman — they were all poor and all hard working people who had established this small, dusty fishing village of Montauk along the great arc of Fort Pond Bay.

After dark, however, when the fishermen were all home in their fishing shacks and tucked in bed, Montauk came alive with an entirely different breed of people. Gun toting desperados, adventurers and city slickers seemed to come out of nowhere to take over the town and, in the darkness, use its docks and beaches for the unloading of bootleg hooch. By dawn's light, these people were gone.

Some said that many of them slept in the woods in the backs of their trucks. Others said that they worked all day too, driving their heavily loaded vehicles into New York City and then back again for another night. Nobody really knew.

Wayne looked at himself in the cracked counter mirror. Large brown eyes, bordered by a shock of curly black hair, stared back at him from under his dirty cap.

"Time to go," he said to Sheila.

Then he reached in his pocket, pulled out a nickel and set it down next to his empty coffee cup.

*   *   *

One half hour later, Wayne Miller was standing at the wheel of the MARY ANNE, piloting it around Rocky Point about half a mile from shore. It was an unusual place to be dropping his lobster pots, but Wayne had figured what the hell, it was an isolated spot and he might as well give it a go. Beneath him, the long-throw Lathrop engine made a sort of banging sound as it pushed the MARY ANNE along. Above, the bright sun shone onto the sea, sending sparkles of sunlight onto the deck.

Wayne unbuttoned his shirt and took it off to reveal a dark, hairy chest and belly. He stretched, yawned and scratched himself. This looks like a good spot he thought.

He turned the ignition off, dropped anchor and walked noisily astern to start dropping his lobster pots. The only other sound he could hear was that of the water slapping against the side of the boat. It was a beautiful summer's day.

*   *   *

And then, there was another sound. From far out at sea he heard the unmistakable whine of a motorboat traveling at very high speed. He looked off to the starboard side of the MARY ANNE and there, off at the horizon he saw a large, black boat heading straight at him. The black boat bounced crazily in the water as it headed toward him, and then Wayne saw that there was not one boat, but two. A second boat, with the colors of the U.S. Coast

Guard was right behind. There were two bright flashes, and then what sounded like two thunder claps.

My God, he thought, they're shooting at each other.

Hurriedly, he grabbed his shirt and ran below. From the galley, he peered through a porthole and continued to watch as a drama slowly unfolded in front of the MARY ANNE.

The large black speedboat came splashing through the water at close to thirty knots, by Wayne's estimate. Men in broadbrimmed hats scurried about, leaned out of hatchways, firing pistols at the Coast Guard boat that was plowing along behind. The Coast Guard ship was gaining.

And then, as the speedboat came within just a few hundred yards of the MARY ANNE, men began appearing on deck with small wooden boxes.

Hooch, Wayne thought.

With a splash, the first of the boxes went over the side. Then another went, another, and another. With each splash, Wayne made a mental note of the exact spot.

Altogether, exactly twenty-two boxes went over the side before the speedboat veered off to port and headed out in an easterly direction. The Coast Guard ship made a turn as well, and came even closer. More shots were fired, and Wayne could see that the Coast Guardsmen were returning the fire now.

In five more minutes, the two boats were nearly as far off on the horizon as they had been when he had first spotted them. But now the ships stopped dead in the water. Off in the distance, he could hear a voice talking over a loud speaker, and he could make out the white figures of the Coast Guardsmen as they boarded the black boat and tied it fast.

* * *

Wayne stayed below in the galley and waited almost an hour until everybody was gone. Then he climbed back up to the wheel of the MARY ANNE and started up the old Lathrop.

Twenty-two boxes. Twenty-two hundred dollars. That's what I'm told anyway.

Carefully, he chugged over and marked each of the twenty-two spots with a lobster pot and a lobster buoy. The buoys made a very strange row in the water, extending for about two hundred yards. He'd have to work fast.

*   *   *

At ten-thirty that morning, the dusty Main Street of Montauk was almost deserted. Wayne walked down this street, past the one-room schoolhouse where the children were chanting in unison inside, past the little Union News magazine store, and past the empty docks where the two dozen fishing boats had been moored only a few hours before.

In the Dockside Cafe, he found Sheila standing in the back, washing the restaurant dishes.

"You using your truck today?" he asked.

"No," Sheila said. "It's okay with me if you want it. But you better check with Pop. How long you need it for?"

"The rest of the day."

"Pop's out back."

Wayne went through the kitchen and found himself outside on the dock by the water's edge. Pop was there, his white hair blowing, naked from the waist up, sitting on a box, shucking clams.

"Howdy, Captain," the old man said, "what brings you here this time of day?"

"Need to use a truck. Sheila says it's all right with her but I'd better check with you."

"What do you need it for and how long?"

"Wanted to go to East Hampton and look at those new Ford automobiles. Thinkin' of buyin' one."

Pop looked up, shading his eyes with his hands.

"You been foolin' around at night?" he asked.

"No. But I may have come into a big inheritance all of a sudden. Got a letter about it this morning."

Wayne shifted from one foot to the other. He wasn't much good at this sort of thing.

Pop's eyes glinted.

"You're lying," Pop said. "But you can use the truck anyway. Just get it back by nightfall and don't give me any more explanin'. The keys are in it."

*　　*　　*

Wayne ducked down low in the driver's seat as he passed the little four room shack on cinderblocks that passed for his home. Still, from under the brim of his cap pulled over his eyes he could see that his wife Agnes was still asleep and probably snoring in the bedroom.

She won't even know I've gone, he thought, as he continued on. The dust, raised by the old truck, obscured his house as he turned onto the paved road by the railroad station.

He drove slowly on, passing the great construction crew at work on the huge Montauk Manor hotel off Edgemere Road, then past the new office building

under construction in a field not far from the Atlantic Ocean.

There was, at this time, a wealthy Miami Beach developer at work in Montauk, building hotels, office buildings and boardwalks in the hopes of creating a summer resort at Montauk similar to the winter resort he also had down in Florida. The developer, a man named Carl Fisher, hoped to have the whole thing open within two years, in time for the summer season of 1929.

He drove on, down the newly paved road leading to the sleepy village of Amagansett, then down Pantigo, finally arriving on the broad Main Street of East Hampton at one P.M. Beautiful old elm trees shaded this lovely busy street, and Wayne, in his fishing clothes and the old black flatbed truck, seemed considerably out of place. He parked behind two fashionable people in a Dusenberg, got out, and walked the few feet into the Baker and Lester Hardware Store.

"I need a few things," he said. "I need a pair of swim fins, two grappling hooks and chains, and an underwater face mask."

The man behind the counter looked at him.

"What are you trying to do? Get some cases of hooch out of the ocean?"

"Nah," Wayne said. "I've got a brother coming to visit. He's a diver, and it's his birthday."

He found himself shifting from one foot to the other again.

Ten minutes later, Wayne parked in front of the East Hampton Town Ford Dealership on Newtown Lane. He got out, rubbed his hands on his pants and went into the glass plated showroom. There, next to a shiny black convertible car, a slender man with a moustache and shiny black hair greeted him with a smile.

"Howdy do," the man said. He walked over. "What can I do for you?"

"I'm interested in a car," Wayne said.

"Well, we've got two kinds, new and used." The man looked him up and down. "Let me show you some of the used."

"Okay."

Out in the back lot, the man with the shiny hair showed him the first of the five used cars that he had there.

"Now this is the least expensive car we've got on the lot," the man said. "But don't let that fool you. It's a Ford and it runs real good."

"What's that pail under the engine?"

"That? Oh, that's the only thing wrong with this particular model. But it's no real bother, really. You just keep this pail right under the engine where it catches all the oil. Then when you want to take 'er out, you just open the hood, take off the oil cap, pour the oil back in from the pail, and then hang the pail on this hook that's been nailed conveniently to the side of the door over here. It's got a little oil leak."

Wayne tugged at his cap.

"Let's talk about that new convertible you've got inside."

"The new CONVERTIBLE," the man said. "Now you're TALKIN'."

*   *   *

Standing on the portside railing of the MARY ANNE, in bathing suit and flippers, Wayne looked left and right. Still nobody around.

He pulled the glass plate mask over his face and then, with a little leap, was off his boat and into the water. This was to be hooch box number nineteen containing Johnny Walker Black Label. Nineteen down and just three to go.

Hours earlier, Wayne had gotten used to the cold

water of the bay. Now he swam around, grabbed a grappling hook, and dove down into the clear water where he could clearly see the next hooch box just five feet from his lobster pot on the bottom of the sea. He wrapped the hook chain around the box, played out the line, and followed it up to the surface. He was spitting water, breathing hard and about to swim with it back to the MARY ANNE when he noticed for the first time that he was not alone. There was the shadow of another boat just to the stern of the MARY ANNE. It seemed to have come out of nowhere.

"What ya doin', Wayne?"

The voice was that of Captain Frank from the dragger boat MONTAUKER, and Wayne looked up to see that that indeed was who it was. Captain Frank stood by the railing.

"Goin' for a swim," Wayne said. "What does it look like I'm doin'?"

"Beats me," Captain Frank said. "I've never seen you go for a swim before."

Wayne dropped the line attached to the grappling hook under water. He could find that later. He moved his face mask up onto his forehead.

"Well, now you know my secret," he said. "I've always liked swimming, but it just seemed like a sissy thing to do. So I've been doing it off the side of my boat."

"I'll be damned," Captain Frank said.

"Hey, Frank, you goin' in now? Do me a favor?"

"Yeah?"

"Tell Agnes I'll be in about seven o'clock. But do me another favor and don't tell her I've been swimming. I'm sort of keeping this as a little private thing, you understand."

"Sure, I understand."

And then Captain Frank disappeared into the little cabin of the MONTAUKER, put the boat in gear and chugged on off.

*   *   *

"You're acting mighty strange," Agnes said as she took the empty dinner plates away from the table. The whole house smelled of their dinner, which had been boiled cabbage.

"I'm going off tonight."

"You're going to WHAT?"

"I'm going OFF. I've got things to do."

"Like what?"

"Things. Money things."

"Wayne, if you're fooling around with those rumrunners, you'll get yourself killed. They've got GUNS."

"I know that."

Agnes did not say anything further. Instead, she turned her back and walked over to the sink to do the dishes. Wayne looked at her, her ripped sweater, her apron wrapped around her broad beam. Silently, he got up from the table and kissed her on the back of the neck.

"Lock the door like you always do," he said. "I'll knock three times. That'll be me."

*   *   *

Wayne closed the front door to his house and heard the bolt click behind him. He waited a moment, let his eyes become adjusted to the darkness, then walked off down Main Street in a westerly direction. In front of him were a few more houses — all bolted and shuttered — the schoolhouse, and then the long arc of the beach leading off into a dense forest.

Indeed, in the stillness of the night, with the crickets chirping loudly all around, he did not have the faintest idea of what he was going to do. All he knew was that he had twenty-two cases of Johnny Walker Black Label locked safely in the hold of the MARY ANNE, and he would have to find a buyer.

He'd have to find one by morning.

Walking along in the dust, he was struck by the stillness of the fishing village around him. Except for an occasional figure, darting furtively between buildings, there was not a soul in sight. The entire town was locked up.

And then, he was aware that someone was walking along with him. He, or she, was about twenty feet off to the right, walking step by measured step with Wayne's progress. Wayne felt for the small fish scaling knife that he had hooked to the belt of his trousers. It would not be much against a revolver. But it was something.

"You lookin' for something?" a male voice said.

"Yeah."

"What?"

"Got something to sell."

"Follow me," the voice said.

Wayne relaxed the grip on his knife, and the figure moved out in front. He could see that it was a rather small, slender man, wearing rough pants, a windbreaker and a felt hat. The figure also appeared to be wearing city shoes.

This small man led him all the way down the arc of the beach, through the woods and onto a trail. After about ten minutes the trail broadened and, amazingly, Wayne began to hear music. He could hear a female singer, a muted trumpet, and an entire jazz orchestra performing one of the popular tunes of the day. How could this be?

The music grew louder and the trail grew broader until an entire nightclub appeared through the trees in the middle of the forest. Wayne stopped in his tracks.

"Come on," the figure said.

There were about sixty people in this nightclub in the woods. There were, perhaps, forty men in suits and twenty women in evening dress, and they all stood talking at a crude, but adequate open air bar that had been set up under a wooden pavillion. A small gasoline driven generator rattled loudly off to one side, powering several strands of lights, some electric lanterns, and the source of the music — an up-to-date Edison phonograph.

"Will you come on?"

Wayne stumbled forward and entered the nightclub, to be greeted with wary smiles on all sides. The drinking and laughing continued, and Wayne watched as the slender man who had led him here talked at the bar with a large man with a cigar in his mouth. This large man walked over.

"You one of the Montauk fishermen?" the man asked.

"Yes."

"Joey here says you've got something to sell. We're having a party here. What is it?"

Wayne swallowed nervously. "Twenty-two cases of Black Label."

The man adjusted his cigar.

"We ain't interested," he said.

"But. . ."

"I said we ain't interested. Listen. Why don't you go back home to your wife and kiddies? You're out of

your league."

"I've got these twenty-two cases."

"Hey, Joey?" the man with the cigar called.

Joey appeared promptly from the bar.

"Yes, boss?"

"Take this fellow out of here. Tell him to forget he was ever here if he knows what's good for him."

"Right, boss."

The slender man motioned to Wayne and led him back out up the path.

"You heard the boss," Joey said.

"Yeah."

The two walked in silence for awhile, until they were well back into the darkness of the woods away from the nightclub. Joey stopped.

"You really want to sell those cases?" he asked.

"Yes."

"Follow me," he said. "I know some people who have a camp up aways. But don't say I told you."

"Okay."

Joey walked on in front now, veered off to the right, and pushed through a narrow trail between some dense underbrush until he was almost to the top of a small hill. Wayne followed along behind.

"I'll leave you now," Joey said. "The people you want are just over the hill."

Almost instantly Joey was gone, leaving Wayne completely alone. He climbed to the top of the rise and then peered down into a small clearing where six men sat around the embers of a campfire. All six men were wearing broadbrimmed hats.

*   *   *

Ten minutes later, Wayne emerged from the underbrush onto the arc of the bay. He was breathing hard and his clothing was ripped and torn from the briars, but he was safe. The men in the broadbrimmed hats had not seen him, had not heard him as he had scampered back down the trail and into the woods.

Wayne stood there on the beach, his hands on his knees, and he stayed there until he had once again caught his breath. But his hands shook, and inside his chest his heart beat at a very rapid rate. He could not just leave the cases in his boat now. He'd have to get rid of them. He'd have to get rid of them somehow before the sun came up in the next few hours.

* * *

In the darkness, Wayne felt his way down the dock to the slip and his MARY ANNE. The man he had seen, the tall figure of a man with what appeared to be a rifle, still stood by the bolted front door of Sheila's Dockside Cafe, watching his progress.

Wayne felt his way on board his boat, fidgeted with some keys and then unlocked the door to the pilot house. Behind him, by the Cafe, he could hear the sound of the rifle clicking.

Wayne turned.

"What do you want?" he shouted nervously into the darkness. "You want this stuff?"

Silently, the figure by the Cafe motioned with his rifle in the direction of the sea. Wayne understood. Quickly, he pulled out the choke, checked that the gears were in neutral, set the spark and turned on the ignition. The MARY ANNE rumbled into life.

Far down the dusty·street, a single lantern light flickered on in the window of a fishing shack.

* * *

Wayne stood on the deck of the MARY ANNE, with the first of the twenty-two boxes cradled in his arms. Behind him were the cliffs of Rocky Point. In front, across fifty yards of water, was the silent hull of a black speedboat.

"I could save you guys a lot of trouble," he shouted.

There was no response.

"Come on over. You'll get 'em anyway. They're all yours."

Again no response.

"All right, then," he said. With one foot on the rail, he heaved the first of these boxes into the sea between himself and the black speedboat. Then he went below to get the second.

* * *

There was the usual crowd of fishermen bustling inside Sheila's Dockside Cafe that morning. Light poured through the open window, mixed with the cigarette smoke and bounced off the cracked mirror at the back of the counter.

At the counter, a very quiet Wayne Miller sat, staring at the cold coffee that he was still stirring in his cup.

"How'd the day go?" someone asked.

"Huh?" Wayne looked up to see Pop, standing by the side of his stool.

"I didn't see ya when ya came in yesterday. How did everything go in East Hampton?"

"Oh, okay."

"You gonna get the Ford?"

"I don't think so, Pop. You know, that Ford we were lookin' at, it looked okay in a magazine. But up close, it just seemed like it would be out of place here in a town like Montauk."

Pop took a puff on a pipe.

"Well," he said, "it would be out of place in the daytime, anyway."

The Potato

People have often asked, passing the many potato fields we've got out here, if the Hamptons have ever grown a really giant potato, larger than any potato grown in Maine or Idaho.

Well, the answer is that as a rule, the Long Island potatoes are about the same size as the Maines, and perhaps a little smaller than the Idahos. But due to heredity, perhaps, there are occasionally true giant Long Island potatoes, which are larger than any potatoes grown anywhere else in the United States.

A number of these giant potatoes get put on display every year. They wind up on the counter in the Agway store in Bridgehampton or in Riverhead, and they are, indeed, a sight to behold. Some of them have been as big as watermelons. But for the very largest potato ever grown on Long Island — and surely it was the largest ever grown in the United States — we have to got back to the year 1892 when a potato was grown in the Springs section of East Hampton that the local residents are still talking about to this day.

The occasion was the International Exposition of 1893 held in Chicago, Illinois, and apparently some

of the sponsors of this event felt a giant potato — one larger than had ever been grown before— would make an impressive exhibit at the Exposition, and would surely be an attraction for the many visitors from foreign countries that would be attending the fair. Naturally, the sponsors turned to Long Island, specifically to one Ferris Talmadge of the Springs. This man, a prominent farmer of the area, was the grandfather of the late Ferris Talmadge Jr., well-known raconteur and local fisherman. The story about the giant potato of Springs comes from the junior Mr. Talmadge, and is told in his local history book TALES OF THE SPRINGS. For all we know, the story may even be true.

The sponsors of the International Exposition of 1893, of course, were smart enough to contact Ferris Talmadge two years ahead. They knew just as well as anybody else that if you're going to grow a giant potato, you've got to put the shaving in the ground well in advance.

Well, Talmadge went out and planted in the spring of 1891. He planted his regular crop of potatoes, and then, taking a special shaving that he had been saving for just such an occasion, he went over to one side of his land and planted it in a pretty large hill. If it was going to be a big potato, it was going to need plenty of room to grow.

Talmadge took special care of the shaving planted in the hill. He covered it with special mulch and fertilizer, and saw that it was watered every day. He was determined he would not let his customers in Chicago down. If it was the biggest potato ever grown they wanted, then it was the biggest potato ever grown they would get.

The fall came, and Talmadge harvested his

regular potato crop. His giant potato, however, he decided to leave in the ground for another year. He could tell by the way the hill was growing that the potato was indeed a big one. Toward spring, as he made his new planting, he wrote the people in Chicago and told them of his progress. He expected he'd be attempting to harvest the giant sometime in the autumn of '92. With any luck, they'd have it in Chicago by the turn of the new year.

Talmadge went out to the hill in September and poked around in the earth with a spade. There was no doubt about it. The giant potato was ready to be dug. The following morning, which was the start of a warm day, he assembled a crew of nine men and took them out to the hill. They all had shovels, and they all commenced to dig. By nightfall, they had gotten a good part of the potato cleared of dirt, but it was rough going. The potato was even bigger than Talmadge thought.

The next day, Talmadge returned with a crew of seventeen, and the day after that he had twenty-one men. About two o'clock in the afternoon of that third day, they finally succeeded in digging that potato. It stood eleven feet wide and sixteen feet long. It was quite an accomplishment to grow one this big. Certainly it was a record.

The biggest wagon in East Hampton was brought up to the potato site the following day, and a team of six horses hitched up. After much work, the workmen were able to dig a deep hole alongside the potato, big enough to back the wagon down into. Carefully, the workmen then pushed the potato down into the hole where it landed with a crash on top of the wagon. They made wagons tough in those days, and this particular wagon was among the toughest. It held the load.

54

Nobody ever knew how those six horses were able to haul that potato wagon out of the hole, but somehow, they did it. A fresh team was called for, and this new team then hauled the giant potato down to the beach at Albert's Landing where it could be loaded on a boat, if there had been one.

Of course, nobody in his right mind wanted to risk his boat in hauling off the record Talmadge potato. Talmadge wrote the people in Chicago and explained the situation, and they wrote back and offered a tremendous amount of money to any fisherman who would like to try to haul the potato off.

Eventually, in the middle of October, a great big coal barge was brought out from the Port of New York, and, with a freighter hauling the lines and keeping it under control, the barge was beached so the potato could be rolled through the surf to it. About half the townspeople in East Hampton participated in this potato rolling, and it was a dangerous business, indeed. On several occasions it appeared that the potato might break loose and just float into the side of the freighter, causing immeasurable damage. But each time the East Hampton men rose to the occasion and got her back under control. After three days, they had her well secured to the barge. These men were well-paid, you may be sure of that.

Nobody quite knows what happened to the potato after it left East Hampton. It certainly was displayed at the International Exposition in Chicago that year of 1893. It was in all the newspapers. The hit of the fair.

But after that? Nobody really knows. It may well have been cut up into the largest portion of french fried potatoes in the history of the world. Perhaps it was mashed with peppers and onions.

For years after the exposition, however, Ferris Talmadge Senior would receive a thousand dollar check in the mail from the enterprising people in Chicago. It came every year in the middle of August, just in time for Talmadge to make his payroll for the harvest. A good many East Hampton people bought homes and raised families on the profits from that one Ferris Talmadge potato.

General Grant's Practical Joke

In 1946, there lived a young man in Washington by the name of Wally Simmons. Wally was a small man, about five-foot-five, with blond hair and blue eyes, but he was bright, had graduated from Princeton, married well, and became a speechwriter in the State Department.

Wally had been in the State Department for nearly three years when the Second World War ended. He had been considered such an excellent writer, had written Department speeches with such clarity and force that he had been consistently exempted from the draft so he could continue his work as a writer.

Wally Simmons was twenty-six years old in the hot summer of 1946. He had a small apartment, a Chevrolet, and a pretty brunette wife by the name of Dorothy. On Friday, August 7, 1946, he was given the most important assignment of his life. The Secretary of State, himself had asked that Wally Simmons write the speech he was scheduled to give at the next Monday morning conference. It was a major policy speech, a dozen different drafts of the speech had already been prepared by lesser officials, and it was to be Wally's job over the weekend to bring the points of all these draft speeches together into one major forceful speech by the Secretary of State.

Wally worked all day Friday at the office on the speech. He brought the rough drafts home with him Friday night and worked all day Saturday and

Sunday. It was a complex assignment. By Sunday night, index cards and notes for the speech were scattered all over the Simmons apartment. There were sections on the kitchen table, notes on the living room floor, even outlines pinned up in the bathroom.

Then, about eleven o'clock Sunday night, just ten hours before the speech was scheduled to be completed, Wally Simmons reached into the breast pocket of his short sleeve shirt for another cigarette. All he found were matches. He tried his pants pockets, and all he came out with were his wallet, thirty-six cents in change, and the receipt from a Chinese laundry. He seemed to be out.

Wally looked under his notes for a pack of cigarettes and couldn't find any. He opened the drawers in the living room desk where the cigarettes were usually kept and saw none. Then he sank back in an overstuffed easy chair.

"Damn," he said.

His wife heard him and came in.

"Is there something wrong, dear?"

"I've got to have a cigarette, and I can't find any. I've got to finish this speech."

"I'll help you look," Wally's devoted wife Dorothy said.

Between them, they spent the next fifteen minutes turning the apartment upside down. It wasn't hard as there were only the three rooms. But no matter where they looked, under the sofa, behind the refrigerator, on the mantel, alongside the bed, they came up empty-handed.

"My God, what am I going to do?" Simmons shrieked.

"I'll drive into town and see what is open," Dorothy said.

"Nothing is open. This whole town goes to bed at ten."

"Maybe SOMETHING is open."

"This is a major policy speech. The whole country depends upon it. What am I going to do?"

It was at this moment that Wally Simmons' eyes lighted upon the one object in the entire apartment that could solve his problem. Sitting on the mantelpiece, inside a sealed glass case, was a nearly one hundred year old cigar, a family heirloom from Dorothy's side of the family. This cigar, together with its case and the explanatory plaque, had been on the mantelpiece of each of the apartments Wally and Dorothy had lived in since they had been married. It was part of the family. The little bronze plaque, mounted above the glass, bore the following inscription:

This Cigar
Was Presented To
Sgt. Harry Armstrong
Of the Eighty-third Infantry
by
GENERAL ULYSSES S. GRANT
During the Parade up Fifth Avenue
in
New York City in May 1866

Wally Simmons stared at the cigar, and an expression of tranquillity came over his face. At first, his wife Dorothy did not know what had come over her husband. But then, following the direction in which her husband was looking, she realized what he saw and her mouth dropped open.

"Wally, NO!"

Wally Simmons rose shakily from his chair and licked his lips. Dorothy threw herself between her husband and the mantelpiece, throwing her arms out in defense of the cigar.

"Wally, the cigar is not ours. It's not ours to smoke. We're supposed to hand it down from generation to generation."

"I know," said Wally, still moving forward.

"Grandpa Armstrong WILLED me that cigar, Wally."

"This is an EMERGENCY."

"Grandfather Armstrong was so overcome with emotion at the sight of General Grant, standing there in the front row of the reviewing stand, that he BROKE RANKS from his regiment, and practically CRAWLED up the steps to the stand to prostrate himself before the General."

"I know, Dorothy."

"And he cried out to the General, 'General Grant, I served under you at Shiloh,' and the General pulled him up, shook his hand and said 'glad to meet you, son,' and he GAVE him that cigar."

Wally Simmons didn't say anything. He had stopped to look for something sturdy with which to break the glass case. He came up with a metal ash tray.

"Wally, for God's sake!"

"Dorothy, that cigar was given to your Grandpa because he had done his patriotic duty. By tomorrow morning, I have got to do MY patriotic duty. I have got to write a major policy speech for the Secretary of State of the United States of America. The future of this entire country may depend upon it. What would your Grandpa Armstrong say if he knew, under these circumstances, that I had to smoke his cigar."

"Oh, my God, Wally," he'd say, "do it, do it."

And she stepped aside.

Wally Simmons stepped forward, shaking, as he

raised the metal ash tray. Then he had shattered the glass, and, hands shaking, picked up the cigar that had not been touched in eighty-six years. Wally licked the end. He put the cigar in his mouth. Then, carefully, he lit the end, inhaled a puff, two puffs, three puffs, and was just beginning to smile with satisfaction when the cigar exploded with a bang right in his face, just as it was supposed to have exploded in Sergeant Harry Armstrong's face eighty-six years earlier.

General Grant was notorious for handing out exploding cigars in those days, though no biographer has ever been able to explain why he did so. What happened that hot August night in 1946 was simply the longest delayed practical joke in history.

The Bonacker
and
The Developer

Not long ago, a big city developer came out to the Hamptons and cast his eyes on a beautiful, vacant piece of woodland up in Springs, East Hampton. After making some inquiries, he found that this land was owned by an old local fellow named Allen, who had inherited the land from his family. The land had been in the Allen family for over a hundred years.

The city developer looked up Allen. He went to his house, a small four-room shack in the woods, surrounded by wrecked automobiles and other junk, and knocked on the door. A woman answered.

"Is Mr. Allen here?"

"Who wants him?"

"My name is Dean. Wesley Fearson Dean III, from New York. My card."

The woman took the card and turned it this way and that.

"Allen's fishing," she said. "He's up in Northwest Creek."

"In a boat?" Dean asked.

"In a boat. You go down this road and make a left. Go up about a mile to a red barn and make a right. About a mile down you'll see a dirt road by a big rock. Turn in there, and you'll come to the creek. He's out there. Just holler. He'll come in. What's this all about?"

"I have a business proposition for Mr. Allen."

"Oh. Well, go see him."

The developer followed directions, called out into the creek, and after a fashion, the old man rowed in.

"Mind if I sit down?" the developer asked.

"Go right ahead. Pull yourself up a gunnel," Allen replied. He was a powerful-looking man, with a leathery face, a yellow cap, and four-day growth of beard. The developer pulled up the tails of his suit jacket and sat.

"I understand you own that two hundred-acre parcel up in the woods."

"Sure do."

"You know it could be worth a lot of money."

"Yep."

"Ever think of developing it?"

"Never thought about it."

"Well, you're zoned one acre up there. You could hire a planner and divide it up into lots. You could plow through and pave a road. Put in drainage, sewer lines, power. You could build a couple of houses at the front of the land. Put up a small office. Do some advertising..."

"All that costs money."

"I could put up the money. That's my business."

"What happens then?"

"Well, we go into partnership, you and I. I'll put up the capital. Probably run about three hundred thousand. You put up the land. It'll be a lot of work. I'll handle it in New York with the attorneys, the promotion, the city advertising. You handle it out here. You know a good builder?"

"Sure do."

"Well, you hire him, get him to put up a couple of houses. You'd handle the asphalting, all the local officials. I wouldn't kid you, it would be a lot of work."

"What happens then?"

"Well, with the money we make selling off the first two houses, we put a down payment on ten more."

"What happens then?"

"We sell those ten, we got the whole thing rolling. We branch out. Set up our own construction business. Hire our own real estate broker to handle the inquiries. Buy some more land."

"What happens then?"

"By then, we'll be making quite a bit of money. We could invest some of the money. Maybe buy a local radio station, or a taxi company. Maybe we buy some more land and develop that."

"What happens then?"

"Well, by that time, if everything was working out all right, we both might be able to take a little time off. We'd be pretty tired by then. I could get in a little more tennis, a little more golf. We could relax. What do you do to relax?"

"Go fishing."

"Well, you could go fishing."

"I am already fishing. As a matter of fact, I thought I saw one jump right over there. If you'll excuse me."

And old man Allen waited until the man was off his gunnel and rowed right back out to the center of the creek.

Sunflower

Mr. Wicker looked out the kitchen window, and he couldn't believe his eyes. There, in the middle of the backyard, about a hundred feet away, was Mrs. Wicker on her hands and knees digging up the lawn. Mr. Wicker went out to look.

"What are you doing?" he asked, when he arrived at the site.

Mrs. Wicker wiggled her broad beam menacingly as she worked.

"I'm making a garden," she said. "I'm turning the earth. That's the first thing you have to do."

"Does the landlord know about this?"

"Certainly. He thought it was a fine idea."

By way of emphasis, Mrs. Wicker stabbed the earth with her little trowel, levered it up, and overturned some deep brown earth wriggling with worms.

"I'm going to make my own salads this summer," Mrs. Wicker continued, stopping to sit back on her haunches. "We're going to have Italian tomatoes and lettuce and peas and cabbage and Brussels sprouts. Carrots, too."

"How do you know?" Mr. Wicker asked suspiciously.

"Because I bought the seeds, you old silly. It says what they are going to be on the packet."

None of this looked very likely to Mr. Wicker. He'd heard about gardens, but in lower Manhattan he'd never seen one up close. He looked at her seed packets, and they were a long way from carrots and tomatoes. He looked back at his fat wife, now back digging merrily away. With her face flushed with sun and exertion, and with a white flowered kerchief tied crookedly around her head, she looked like a Russian peasant in a magazine. A big, broad-beamed woman digging up the Ukraine for potatoes and Socialism. It would be her first garden in nearly forty years of marriage. She looked very happy. Mr. Wicker rolled up the copy of the New Yorker in his thin hands behind his back, and thought that maybe it wasn't so bad his wife had talked him into renting the summer house. But he wondered if she wasn't wasting her time with this garden business.

The following week, after Mr. Wicker had punched the timeclock ending his day in the bookkeping department of Osborne and Fitch, Investments, after he had gone back to the apartment, changed and packed for the weekend, after he had taken the subway up and the train out to East Hampton, after his wife Hilda had met him, taken him home and fed him, after a good night's sleep in the big bedroom that smelled of the leaves, and after a big breakfast of orange juice, bacon, pancakes and coffee, he went back out into the backyard to see how his wife was doing. It was Saturday.

"What do you think?" Hilda asked, standing alongside the garden proudly.

Mr. Wicker looked down. In the ground in front of him was a small brown rectangle of earth, about two feet wide and four feet long. It didn't look very big for growing tomatoes and carrots and peas and whatever else it was she was going to grow.

Furthermore, there WAS nothing growing. All there was in this space was a variety of wooden sticks in the ground announcing there would be CARROTS, or BRUSSELS SPROUTS or LETTUCE. White string connected one stick to another in an apparently well-thought-out pattern, and there was a fence of chicken wire crookedly surrounding the project. It was pretty ugly.

"Very nice," was what Mr. Wicker said.

"You still look suspicious," Hilda said smiling. "You still look like you can't imagine anything growing here. Well, you'll see. It is still June. By the end of the summer, you'll be eating salads made in my very own garden. You really will."

"And they'll be the best-tasting salads in the whole world," Mr. Wicker said expansively.

"Organic, too," Mrs. Wicker said.

The weeks went by. Nothing appeared. Then, one Saturday morning, Mr. Wicker was sent into town to buy some sixty-watt light bulbs. Three had burned out, and Hilda had been snatching bulbs from lamp to lamp as they settled in one part of the house or another.

Mr. Wicker walked into the little country hardware store, and a bell tinkled over the door. He looked around. Hardware supplies were arranged in avalanche fashion on both sides of him. There were garden hoses, screws and nuts, lawn mowers, plastic garbage can covers, and lanterns dangling menacingly on both walls. And there was a huge display of seed packets. Mr. Wicker looked at the display, at the beautiful flowers and vegetables pictured on the front of the little white packages. And he thought of the garden in the back.

"Can I help you?"

Mr. Wicker looked up. The voice came from a big

bald man with hairy arms crossed on top of a big belly. He stood behind a counter next to a display of grass seed.

"Three sixty-watt light bulbs," Mr. Wicker said.

The man went to some shelves and looked.

"We're fresh out," he said. "How about some seventy-fives?"

"Fine."

"You want frosted or soft light?"

"Either one. Frosted, I guess."

"They come in packets of four."

"That's okay."

The hardware store man put the bulbs in a bag, and Mr. Wicker paid for them. But then, the two men just stood there in silence.

"Something else I can get you?"

"I was wondering," Mr. Wicker said, "about growing flowers."

"What about them?" the man said. He brushed some imaginary hair back on his bald head.

"What's the biggest flower they make, I mean, that you can grow from a seed around here."

"Oh, I guess the sunflower must be about the biggest."

"How big?"

The hardware store man held his hand out chest high.

"This big," he said.

"And how big is the flower?"

The man formed his fingers into a circle the size of a dinner plate.

"Like that."

The hardware store man walked from behind the counter over toward the seeds.

"You want a pack?"

"How long would it take to grow? I mean, would

there be a flower by the beginning of August?"

"Certainly."

"Then I'll take one."

The man handed Mr. Wicker the packet of sunflower seeds.

"No, just one. One seed."

"One seed? The whole packet is just twenty cents."

"That's okay. I just want one seed."

"I'll have to break open the packet. Charge you the full twenty cents."

"I'll pay it," Mr. Wicker said. "Sell the rest to somebody else."

The hardware store man shrugged and took the packet over to the counter by the cash register. Then he ripped a small hole in one corner and carefully poured out one large, wedge-shaped seed. He held it out in the palm of his hand. It was larger than a pea. And it was going to grow into a sunflower.

Half an hour later, after changing the light bulbs, Mr. Wicker walked out into the yard and over toward the garden. He studied it for a moment, then walked around to the side farthest from the house. There, in the one-inch space between the edge of the garden and the chicken wire, he got down on his hands and knees and pressed the seed into the grass and down under the ground about four inches. He hoped he hadn't hurt it.

"What's this all about?" the voice behind him said.

Mr. Wicker looked and saw a broad shadow on the lawn, arms on its hips, then followed it back to the shoes of his wife standing over him.

"Oh, a surprise," he said. "I've planted something."

"What?"

"I told you. It's a surprise. It'll grow, and you'll see."

Mr. Wicker scrambled to his feet, looking slightly upward into the eyes of his wife. She looked apprehensive, and he wondered if he really should have been tampering with her garden.

"It's a surprise," he repeated rather feebly.

The days passed and Mr. and Mrs. Wicker settled into a routine together. Every Friday Mr. Wicker would arrive from his work at the investment company, and every weekend he would inspect the progress of the garden, which had begun to grow. Sunday nights he took the train back to the City.

A first, there were just sprouts, little delicate blades of green emerging from the ground, pointing hopefully at the sky. Then there were shoots and leaves and more sprouts, until the tiny rectangle was literally thatched with an orderly display of growing things. Hilda happily pointed out which were tomatoes and which were carrots, and although they didn't look anything like vegetables to Mr. Wicker, he supposed that it was so, and was impressed with what was taking place.

It was at the back of the garden, away from the house, however, that the most dramatic things began to happen. There, among the weeds that grew between the garden and the chicken wire — and Mr. Wicker forbade Hilda to pick those weeds for fear of ruining his surprise — there arose a large, hairy green plant that seemed to resemble, more than anything else, the beanstalk in Jack and the Beanstalk. Mr. Wicker supposed it was the sunflower, but he really wasn't sure. It grew a foot high, then two feet, then four. It literally towered over the rest of the garden, but still, until it became a sunflower — and Mr. Wicker was sure he would recognize a sunflower — only then could he be completely sure.

Then one Sunday morning at about eleven o'clock, Mr. Wicker was in the living room reading the book section of the Sunday New York Times, when he heard Hilda shriek in the back yard.

"Oh! Come quick!" she shouted.

Mr. Wicker ran to the back door, banging the screen door behind him, and was out beside her in a moment.

"Look!" she said. "It's a sunflower! Oh, my goodness!"

Hilda turned and hugged her husband, almost crushing him in her arms. She smelled of ammonia and dish soap. Over a shoulder, Mr. Wicker caught a peep of the magnificent sunflower: a single yellow burst of a flower with long, slender, sunny petals darting foward and out. It was so big, it seemed nearly a miracle on its slender green stem.

Then, in September, the garden, and the sunflower with it, began to die. The petals of the flower turned darker, drooped, and then feel off. As the leaves in the garden withered, the black eye of the sunflower also turned, slowly disintegrating to the ground. All that remained was the huge stem, four feet high, almost up to Mr. Wicker's shoulders.

When the lease ran out, at the beginning of October, it still stood, and showed little signs of age.

"I'm going to cut the sunflower stalk down," Hidla Wicker said as she rolled up the chicken wire. They would be leaving the following day.

"Don't cut it," Mr. Wicker said. "It'll kill it."

"Oh no, it won't."

"Look how tall it is. It grew that high in that short a time. That was so much work. Surely you can't cut something down that grew like that without hurting it."

"It's like corn. It comes and it goes. It will be back."

"I think it is going to be a tree," Mr. Wicker said.

In the end, they let it stand. As they drove out of the driveway that last Sunday, the car packed to the door handles with suitcases and boxes, Mr. Wicker stopped and looked back at the tall sunflower that still stood in the yard. The house was not going to be rented out the next summer as the landlord would be using it himself. Mr. Wicker wondered if the sunflower would still be there in the spring, and if it was, if the landlord would like it or cut it down. Maybe they ought to leave him a note about it.

But then he turned frontwards and stepped on the gas, and they were out of the driveway toward the setting sun, and the third floor apartment in lower Manhattan.

Cecil Pontopolis

The two old ladies, sitting in their aluminum folding chairs on the beach, could hardly believe their eyes. There, not a hundred yards from them, on the other side of the lifeguard stand, sat a man in a bathing suit who looked exactly like Cecil Pontopolis.

"I really think that's him," the lady in the big yellow sunhat said, trying not to look like she was looking at him.

"No, it couldn't be," the other lady replied. "Cecil Pontopolis is one of the richest men in the world. What would he be doing here, in EAST Hampton. The very richest men always go to SOUTHampton."

"Well, he looks exactly like his pictures in the movie magazines," the first lady said. "Anyway, it's the beginning of the season. Maybe Mr. Pontopolis is starting a trend toward East Hampton.

"The BILLIONAIRES will NEVER come to East Hampton," the second lady said with authority.

Marvin Levine, the twenty-year-old Fordham College junior, working as the lifeguard on the beach that day, already knew that it was Cecil Pontopolis. Sitting up there, high on his lifeguard stand, he had already heard Mr. Pontopolis' butler addressing the billionaire by his name. Mr. Levine had a vision that he would rescue the apple juice billionaire sometime that day, and thereupon be financially independent for the rest of his life, but he knew that this would never actually happen. He had already seen Pontopolis swim, a surprisingly strong swimmer for a man in his middle fifties. And then Levine remembered that the billionaire had once been on the American Olympic swimming team in his younger days. At least, so the newspapers said.

Cecil Pontopolis was naturally oblivious to all this

business with the two ladies and the lifeguard. He was much more involved with the business at hand, which was lying on the sand, listening to the sound of the sea, watching the gulls, and reading back issues of the Saturday Evening Post. It was there, in a back issue published in 1952, that he had read East Hampton was the most beautiful village in the United States. It had been selected as such by the editors of the magazine. Mr. Pontopolis had been so impressed when he had read this just three months ago, that he had driven out from his office in the city, saw that the place was indeed as beautiful as the magazine had said, and had thereupon arranged to buy the fifty-two room estate on Georgica Pond. Mr. Pontopolis also had stacks of back issues of the Reader's Digest and National Geographic, the other two publications that gave him pleasure, stacked up in the sand. Neither of them, however, had ever mentioned anything about East Hampton.

A tall, thin man of about forty-five came out of the surf and walked up toward Mr. Pontopolis. Harry, the butler. Well, I guess I won't be rescuing him either, Marvin Levine thought.

"How was it?" Cecil asked, looking up from an

issue with a picture of Franklin Roosevelt on the front.

"Bracing," Harry said. He grabbed a velour towel. "I think it's still a bit early in the season, for me anyway."

"Shall we go?" Cecil asked. It was already three o'clock in the afternoon.

"If you wish, sir. I've had quite enough."

Cecil got up as Harry, the butler, dried himself with the towel. They gathered up their things, Cecil taking the ice bucket, the beach blanket and the portable TV, while Harry staggered under the weight of fifty issues of back magazines. Cecil had a date that evening with Princess Adreanne von Hapsburg, a resident of Southampton and Cecil's newest flame, at least according to Women's Wear Daily.

"I'm SURE that's him," the old lady in the floppy yellow sunhat stated with finality as the two men disappeared with their beach gear over the dune toward the parking lot.

*　*　*

The big Irish policeman waddled over to the two men as they were loading the beach equipment into the trunk of the convertible sports car.

"So that's YOUR car," the policeman said, sweating in his heavy blue policeman's uniform. "That's SOME car."

The two men stopped and looked up.

"Yes, it's handmade," Cecil said. "It was made in Milan by Sergio Ferrari himself. It's the only one like it in the world.

"Well, it's SOME car."

The policeman patted gently on its metallic grey trunk.

"Would you like a ride in it?" Cecil asked.

"I sure would."

"Hop in. Harry, we'll be right back," Cecil said

to Harry, who was still standing there holding the back issues of the magazines.

Cecil got behind the wheel, and the fat policeman squeezed in on the passenger's side.

"Say," the policeman said, "aren't you Cecil Pontopolis, the famous billionaire?"

The policeman extended his hand.

"I'm glad to meet you. I'm Pat O'Flaherty of Three Mile Harbor."

They shook hands across the stick shift. Cecil pressed a button, and the automobile started with a great roar. Then it settled down to a quiet idle, like a patient stallion. Cecil pushed the clutch in, threw the gearshift toward the dashboard, and the gleaming sports car surged forward down the road. They passed a pretty girl in a bikini walking by the side of the road and they beeped as they went past. Everybody smiled and waved. Then Cecil noticed the yellow tag stuck down under the windshield wiper.

"What is that?" Cecil asked.

"Oh, THAT?" O'Flaherty said. "That's a ticket. A parking ticket. You don't have a parking sticker you know and you have to have one. That's why I'm down at the beach. Writing up parking tickets."

"Oh," Cecil said.

"Boy, this is SOME car," O'Flaherty said, hanging onto his hat as they ripped around a corner. Cecil took the policeman down one little road and then down another, passing potato fields and summer mansions, not quite as large and not quite as numerous as those in Southampton. Cecil thoroughly enjoyed driving his handmade sports car, and he especially enjoyed driving it with someone who appreciated it, as this East Hampton policeman certainly did.

After they got back to the parking lot, O'Flaherty got out of the car and thanked him profusely for the ride.

"You want me to tear up that parking ticket, Mr. Pontopolis?" O'Flaherty said. "No, I guess you wouldn't want me to do that. I couldn't do that anyway. I've got a carbon and they're all numbered and I've got to account for them. Besides, you're a billionaire. It's only five dollars."

"You're only doing your job," Cecil said. He wasn't mad.

Cecil and Harry piled back into the car, and they drove the half mile to the house by the pond. Harry piled out with the magazines, and then the ice chest, the portable TV, and the beach blanket. Cecil put on a white silk shirt over his bathing suit, and drove off to go into town. He had decided to settle his parking ticket and get a sticker all at the same time at the Village Hall on Main Street.

"I'm sorry, but you can't pay the five dollars here, Mr. Portuckulis," the blue-haired lady behind the counter said at Village Hall.

"Mr. Pontopolis," Mr. Pontopolis said.

"Mr. Pontopolis. Say, are you THE Mr. Pontopolis?"

"Yes."

"Well, you'll STILL have to wait for the ticket to be processed, just like anyone else," the lady said condescendingly.

"That's just fine."

"You'll get a bill in the mail."

"How about getting a parking sticker for me so this won't happen again?"

The blue haired lady sighed. It was already four o'clock and they were supposed to be closing. But she turned to the tax file, listing everyone in the village, and began to look through the "P's."

"There is no Portuckulis," she said finally.

"Pontopolis. Pontopolis."

The lady looked some more.

"There isn't anybody by that name either." She folded her arms.

"But I live in East Hampton."

"Perhaps you live in the Township. This is the Village."

The lady turned and went into a back office labeled ASSESSORS OFFICE. Through the door, Cecil could see an older man looking at the tax maps for Mr. Pontopolis's parcel. The woman returned.

"It IS in the Township. It's out of the Village limits by about fifty feet. You can get a green sticker and you can get a red sticker, but you can't get a yellow sticker."

"What's the difference?" Cecil asked.

"With the green sticker you can use the Township beaches. That's ten dollars. With the red sticker you can use the Township beaches and two of the Village beaches. But you can't use three of the other Village beaches."

"What about the beach where I got this ticket?"

"That's one of the restricted village beaches. You have to be a resident of the Village. And you have to have a yellow sticker. You can't buy that because you're not a resident. Not even for a billion dollars."

"But that's a nice beach. And it's the nearest beach with a lifeguard to my home."

"Well, that's the way it is, Mr. Pontuckulus. By

the way, there is a law in this village that you can't wear shorts more than midway above the knee. I just thought I'd warn you. We don't enforce it, though."

Cecil scratched his head in wonder, walked out to the street and got in his car. Then he went home and got dressed for his date with Princess Adreanne von Hapsburg, the true light of his life. This season, anyway.

The following Tuesday, Cecil Pontopolis drove into New York City. Cecil did not particularly like leaving his big home in East Hampton during the summer, but once every week he had to make an appearance in Manhattan to sign some checks. And once every month he had to preside over a major policy meeting. This particular Tuesday was the day of that monthly meeting.

Cecil took the Ferrari out of the garage, and, deliberately avoiding the Expressway, took the twisting, winding, back country roads toward the city. It was good exercise for the car, and under the warming sun, it was good exercise for Cecil. His white hair flying, he arrived at the Queens-Midtown Tunnel in just under an hour and fifty minutes. Ten minutes later, he pulled his car to a stop in front of a fifty-five story building on Lexington Avenue. It was a hot day.

"Good morning, Mr. Pontopolis," the doorman said. "Harvey will be right out."

Cecil nodded and smiled, and stepped out of his car into the street. He had parked the car, temporarily, in a no-parking zone.

Harvey came out of the building, a tall, thin young man in garage overalls.

"Good morning, Mr. Pontopolis," he said in his Italian accent, as Cecil handed him the keys.

"Good morning, Harvey. She's running beautifully. But there is a rattle in the left front wheel."

"I'll go over it from stem to stern, sir."

Cecil entered the huge, marble lobby, with its half-dozen sculptures of apples and apple trees, and walked toward the bank of elevators, passing the young woman manning the reception desk.

"Why, Mr. Pontopolis," she said. "Good MORNING. Would you care for some apple juice?"

"Don't mind if I do," Cecil said.

The receptionist pressed a small silver button and a small, chrome apple juice dispenser rose out of a panel in the desk. Automatically, the dispenser produced a cup, the cup was quickly filled, and the cup, on a small metal tray, swung out toward Cecil's waiting hand. As he brought the cup quickly to his lips, then tasted the refreshing cold drink as it soothed his dry mouth, parched from the long drive, he thought of the thousands of acres of apple trees in Wisconsin, in Iowa, in Pennsylvania and Nebraska, the factories in five major cities, the skyscrapers, the handmade Ferrari, and the house on the beach. Cecil never turned down an offer of apple juice.

Two hours later, on the fifty-third floor, after a series of meetings in which he had sold one factory and bought two, Cecil retired to the small office of Jack Brady, the wily old accountant, who had been with him since the first bottle of apple juice in the cellar of his parents' house in Milwaukee, Wisconsin.

"How do you think it went?" Cecil asked, leaning back in a small chair, and putting his feet up on Brady's cluttered desk.

"I think we're going to make a lot of money with that factory in Argentina," Brady said. "Incidentally, here is the first of our summer apples from our new orchard in California."

Brady handed Cecil a bright red apple.

"I didn't know we had an orchard in California," Cecil said.

"It's new. Not far from San Francisco. We've had it about a month and a half."

Cecil took a big crunching bite of the apple, and looked out the window at the smog of lower Manhattan as he savored the taste.

"Not bad," he said. "Want some?"

"No, thanks," Brady said, waving a short stubby arm. "An apple is an apple, I always say."

"So you do."

"How was your trip in? How do you like your new house?"

"The trip was fine. The house is fine. We got a little problem out there, though. It seems the house is about fifty feet outside the Village limits. That nice beach I wanted to go to is restricted to Village residents only. You need a car sticker. I've gone there four straight days now, and this policeman, O'Flaherty, has given me four straight tickets. The fine on each ticket is double the one before. The last ticket was forty dollars."

Brady winced.

"Any chance their moving the Village limits?"

"I don't think so. I suppose I'll have to buy some property inside the Village. Either that, or just have Harry drop me off every day."

Brady thought about that.

"The fines double with every ticket?" he asked.

"That's right."

"What's the limit?"

"I don't think there is one."

"I've been meaning to tell you this, Cecil, but you need a big tax write off."

"How big?"

"Ten or twenty million. The trouble is, everything you touch tends to MAKE money. I've been having a hard time trying to find something we could lose this money on. This fine business sounds foolproof."

"I think it is."

At that moment, Max Werner, the vice president in charge of production, stepped into the office.

"That fellow from the East Coast Bottling Company is here," Werner said to Brady.

"Oh, yes. We're going out to lunch. Tell him I'll be out in a minute. Cecil, how about joining us? We're going out to the Tavern on the Green. I'm sure he'd appreciate meeting you."

"No, thanks," Cecil said. "To tell you the truth, during this entire morning of meetings, I've been thinking of nothing but a great big pizza pie. With pepperoni."

"Be my guest," Brady said, pressing a button on his desk. A secretary came in.

"Get this man a large pizza with pepperoni," Brady said.

"For Mr. Pontopolis?"

"Yes," Cecil said. "And a big, cold, glass of apple juice."

* * *

Mayor Breckinridge always had trouble with his air conditioner. Whenever he turned it up, within twenty minutes he was freezing to death. Then, when he turned it back down, he'd start to sweat. There didn't seem to be an operable thermostat in the thing, but the three times that he had gotten a repair man to look at it, and just GETTING the repairman had been a major proposition, it had been returned in a few days sporting a clean bill of health, which proved inaccurate. The Mayor had, at one meeting of the Board of Supervisors of East Hampton, suggested that perhaps they get a new air conditioner for his office, but at that meeting his proposal had been voted down unanimously. It was an election year, and the last thing anybody wanted was to make the tax rate go up. The Mayor would have to struggle along.

The door opened, and Albert Baker, treasurer for the Village of East Hampton, came in.

"Brrrr. It's cold in here," Baker said.

The Mayor got up and turned down the air conditioner. Then he blew his nose. He had a pretty bad cold.

Baker set a few papers down on the Mayor's desk.

"Have a look at these," Baker said.

The Mayor looked.

"So we have the great apple juice billionaire in town," he said, "and he gets parking tickets. So what?"

"Look at the amounts."

The Mayor looked again. There was a total of ten tickets in ten days and each fine was double the one before. The fine for the tenth ticket was $2,500.

"Mr. Pontopolis really likes to go to the beach," the Mayor said.

"In the last ten days, the fines of Mr. Pontopolis have totalled $5,115. That's more than all our other parking fines for the week put together."

Mayor Breckinridge didn't say anything.

"Do you realize what these fines will be, if they keep doubling for another three or four days?" Baker asked.

"No, can't say that I do."

"We figure that if he goes to the beach tomorrow, Friday, Saturday and Sunday, then on Monday his fine will be $81,920."

The Mayor blinked. That amount represented all the money they made from all the parking fines at the beach all summer.

"You don't think he'll do that," the Mayor said, adjusting his tie. "He's probably just figuring on going to the beach for a few days like this. I mean, he may be a rich man and all, but he's not STUPID."

"Well, I just wanted you to know about this,"

Baker said, putting all the papers back together.

"They're all at the same beach, aren't they?" the Mayor said.

"The one near his home."

"Hmmm."

Baker picked the papers up, put them under his arm, and went out the door. The Mayor thought for a moment, then got up, went to the window, and turned the air conditioner back to high.

Tuesday morning was warm and clear, and about eleven o'clock Cecil Pontopolis decided to go to the beach. He changed into his bathing suit, ordered Harry to load some back magazines into the trunk of the Ferrari, and then telephoned Princess Adreanne von Hapsburg in Southampton.

"OF COURSE I'll go to the beach with you. I'd LOVE to," she said.

"I'll be over to pick you up in fifteen minutes," Cecil said.

"Why don't I drive over and meet you THERE, dah-ling?"

"You can't, pussycat. You'll get fined if you park over here. You need an East Hampton parking sticker."

"I read where YOU don't have an East Hampton parking sticker."

"You READ that?"

"In the Southampton Summer Day. It says you're paying a zillion dollars worth of parking fines because you don't have a parking sticker."

"That's a silly paper, pussycat. You know you can't believe anything you read in there."

"Well, that's what it said, dah-ling."

"I'll be over in fifteen minutes, Adreanne."

"I'll be waiting."

Princess Adreanne von Hapsburg was sitting on the front porch of her gleaming Southampton estate, left to her by her last husband. When Cecil pulled up the drive, she stood up to her full six-feet-one, waved excitedly, and then ran like a little girl down to the waiting Ferrari. She was wearing a see-through knit robe, and under it the skimpiest tiny white bikini imaginable. She looked, as they say, smashing. Reaching the car, she folded herself up with surprising grace, slipped into the small seat, and tucked her knees up to her chin.

"You didn't bring any of those damn Saturday Evening Posts to read, did you, dah-ling?" she asked Cecil, who was holding the door for her.

"Of course I did, pussycat."

Ten minutes later, the Ferrari roared into the small parking lot at the back of the East Hampton beach. There were only about six cars there at that hour during the week, but there was Pat O'Flaherty, sitting in his patrol car, apparently waiting for the arrival of Cecil Pontopolis.

Cecil pulled the Ferrari into a parking space, and O'Flaherty was out of his police car as if shot from a gun. He waddled over, and Cecil could see that he was sweating more heavily than ever before.

"Hi," the policeman said with great familiarity. He had, after all, given Cecil sixteen straight tickets. "Who's your friend?"

The princess had gotten out on the passenger side and, standing at her full height, she could look down on the top of O'Flaherty's blue flannel police hat.

"This is Princess Adreanne von Hapsburg," Cecil said, opening the trunk of the Ferrari.

Disconcerted, the policeman bowed.

"How do you do, princess," he said. "I'm Pat O'Flaherty of Three Mile Harbor."

"Pleased to meet you."

The princess extended a limp right hand and Pat O'Flaherty stared at it. Eventually, he shook it.

"You know what the fine is today?" the policeman said to Cecil, finally getting down to business. "You know what it is? I'll tell you what it is. It's a hundred and sixty-three thousand dollars to park here today. At least that's what Mayor Breckinridge told me." O'Flaherty was fidgeting rapidly with the parking ticket book he held in his left hand and the pencil he held in his right.

"I thought you said you couldn't believe anything you read in that paper," the princess said.

Cecil shrugged.

"I've got to get this very carefully," O'Flaherty said. "I musn't make a mistake." The policeman walked to the rear of the car, where Cecil stood, and then squatted on his haunches not six inches from the license plate, effectively taking up all the room at the rear of the car. Cecil had gotten the towels, the ice chest, and the other paraphernalia, but now he couldn't reach the magazines. The princess stood with her hands on her hips, tapping her foot.

"Do me a favor, Mr. O'Flaherty," Cecil said. "When you're done, please close the trunk."

"Seven, three, eight...now you've broken my train of thought. Look. The ticket will be on the windshield. There's a slight breeze, so I'm going to Scotch Tape it there, okay?"

"Okay," Cecil said. He walked around the car, took Adreanne's hand, and then walked over the dune, through the warm sand, and down toward the lifeguard stand. A great many heads on the beach turned. But Cecil had seen this before and he attributed it more to Adreanne than to anything he might have done.

* * *

The following evening, at eight o'clock, the people of East Hampton assembled at the Village Hall to consider the annual budget for the following year. Ordinarily, about fifteen or twenty citizens were interested enough in the fate of their tax money to sit through this lengthy meeting, but on this night the hall was packed to the rafters. Word had gotten around, through the newspapers, over the radio, from neighbor to neighbor, that an "extraordinary income" had already taken place that nearly doubled the annual budget for the year. Furthermore, it appeared very likely that there was more to come.

Mayor Breckinridge started the meeting promptly at eight and, after the reading of the minutes of the previous meeting, the treasurer's report, and the planning committee report, he got to the business at hand immediately.

"I think you all have in front of you the mimeographed sheets which indicate the various cost proposals for the coming fiscal year," the Mayor said, sitting majestically under the Village Seal on the wall. "And I think you can see that with this proposed budget, there will be ABSOLUTELY NO TAX INCREASE FOR THE COMING YEAR WHATSOEVER."

The Mayor sat up and grinned, and he looked left and right, where the other four members of the Village Board sat flanking him, smiling and nodding as well.

"Now, as many of you know," the Mayor continued, "within the last week we have had an extraordinary income from the parking tickets obtained by the apple juice millionaire, Cecil Pontopolis. As of last night, these tickets totalled $330,235 in fines."

"Have these fines been paid?" someone asked from the audience.

"Some of them," the Mayor said. "We've billed out $5,115 and it was paid almost immediately. I have no doubt he will pay the rest. I would also appreciate it if you would not speak out of turn. Raise your hand and I'll recognize you. Now, today, I understand, he received another parking ticket, the fine for which is $327,680. Is that correct?" The Mayor looked at Officer O'Flaherty, who stood, arms folded, guarding the door.

"That is correct," the officer said. "I gave it to him at eleven twenty-six this morning.

"Now, the question is," the Mayor continued, "what are we going to do with all this extra money? It now totals almost $660,000. I will entertain suggestions from the floor."

Three hands went up and the Mayor, to start things off, immediately recognized the real estate and hotel owner, Ted Walker. Walker stood up to his height of five-feet-seven, ran his fingers over his bald head, and looked around him at his friends and neighbors.

"This money that is coming in," Ted began, "is really found money. We wouldn't have had it otherwise, and we never would have counted on it. I propose we do something very special with it, namely, that we build the biggest and finest beach pavillion eastern Long Island has ever seen. Six-hundred and sixty thousand dollars is a great deal of money and it will go a long way. I think people will come from great distances to use the beach pavillion, and the money they will bring in, why, I think it will benefit us all." Ted glanced down at some notes he had in his hand. "The money came from the beach, let's return it to the beach," he said. And then he sat down. There was no applause, and about three or four people hissed lightly. Bringing a whole lot of people out to the beach was not going over too well.

The Mayor recognized Lillian Tattersall, a tall, slim young woman, who had a Ph.D. and was teaching English Literature at Southampton College.

"You all know me," Lillian began, "and you all know where I stand regarding this money, or ANY money that the Village might receive. Development is wrong. Whether it be for a new beach pavillion, or new apartment houses, or new curbs and sidewalks, the development of East Hampton Village beyond its present size is not to be desired by human beings. There are animals living here. Trees and flowers. I propose that if there is ANYTHING done with this money, and I'm not so sure that it should be, then it should be used for the purchase of open land for the creation of undeveloped parks and game preserves. That would do more good for East Hampton Village than anything else."

Dr. Tattersall sat down amid a scattering of applause. The Mayor and the four Village councilmen sat silently at the front, hands stroking their chins in the attitude of the wise men that they had been selected to be. Mayor Breckinridge recognized Frank Deerfield, the well-known local building contractor.

Deerfield stood up, a small, fat man, and puffed on his cigar, in full disregard of the NO SMOKING sign.

"What have we got now, $660,000?"

"That's right."

Everyone could see the wheels turning and the adding machine clicking behind the thick wet cigar.

"Today is Wednesday. Tomorrow, he comes in with a parking ticket worth half a million dollars, Friday, a million, and Saturday, two million. That's four million dollars. You know what that will buy? That, for starters, will get matching funds from the State, and then matching funds again from the federal government. For sixteen million dollars we can have that superhighway bypass we've been talking about but not doing anything about for the last three years. We'll get all those cars off the Montauk Highway. No more trucks downtown, holding up things at the traffic lights. That's what we ought to do with this money. And we ought to do it FAST."

Deerfield sat down and there was complete silence. Nobody had really thought very far ahead. Four million dollars worth of parking tickets?

"The Board will take these three proposals under consideration," the Mayor said, "and I think we will present our decision at the next regularly scheduled meeting, which happens to be this Friday. That would be the day of Mr. Pontopolis's first million dollar parking ticket, and I think we could then know if we could go ahead with a planned bypass or not. Now, before we go ahead with the next part of our meeting, which is a discussion of the size of the lightbulbs to be used in our new street lights, I would just like to add one more proposal for the use of this new money, and that is the purchase of a new air conditioner for the Mayor's office. Now, as most of you know. . ."

The major issue was over, and as the Mayor continued, there was a great rumbling of chairs as almost everyone got up, walked down the aisles and made for the exits. The meeting on Friday would be quite interesting.

* * *

Harry Walker looked at the clock on the post office wall. It was ten after one. He mopped his brow with the handkerchief he kept in his pocket, and noticed that his hand was shaking. Why should he be nervous? He had been Postmaster for twenty-two years, and he never felt this way before. It was only a letter. The sun streamed through the venetian blinds. A good number of patrons had come into the little lobby in their bathing suits. It seemed impossible that Pontopolis had not gone to the beach and received the parking ticket.

Walker waited on an older woman who complained about a pornographic flyer she had received in her post office box. He had her fill in a form. Then he turned and walked toward the small office with the bronze plaque reading HARRY WALKER, POSTMASTER on the door, with the idea in mind to call Mayor Breckinridge again, when he looked up and there was Mayor Breckinridge standing at the counter, pale as a ghost.

"Here it is, Harry," the Mayor said, extending a small yellow envelope.

Harry took the envelope and set it down on the counter. With his twenty-two years of experience, he examined it professionally.

"The stamp seems all right."

"You sure you don't need a twenty-cent stamp? I could put another nickel on it."

"No, fifteen cents is fine. You only need fifteen cents when you mail a letter to East Hampton. I only take it from one part of the post office to another."

Harry looked at the letter again. The return address was good. The address, to Cecil Pontopolis, Box 13145, East Hampton, 11937, was typed without error. Inside would be a bill for that morning's parking ticket, a ticket costing one million, three hundred ten thousand, seven hundred twenty dollars. The Village was billing by the day.

"Well, here goes," said Harry. He picked up the letter.

"You don't mind if I watch, do you?" the Mayor asked.

"No, not at all."

Harry turned and let the Mayor in behind the counter, then led him around to the side of the bank of post office boxes where the Pontopolis box was located. Harry dropped the letter on the floor and it skittered under a table.

"YOU DAMN FOOL!" the Mayor shouted before he could stop himself.

Harry bent down under the table and picked up the letter. Then he glared at the Mayor. He wasn't nervous now. He knew exactly what he was doing. Among the wooden egg crate of the post office boxes, he found the crayon lettering marked Box 13145, and deftly pushed the letter into the cubicle under it.

"You sure it doesn't go into the cubicle OVER the lettering?" the Mayor asked.

Harry looked at the Mayor and there was fire in his eyes. He should never have given him permission to come behind the counter in the first place.

*   *   *

At that very moment, as Harry Walker was placing the first million dollar parking ticket bill into Cecil Pontopolis's mail box, Mr. Pontopolis was swimming forty yards off shore in the Atlantic Ocean. Every stroke he was taking must be costing at least a thousand dollars, he thought, but then, if that's what Brady wanted, then that's what they would do. It amused him that government tax laws were often so complicated, and it amused him even further that the lifeguards, and there were now THREE of them crowded up on top of the rickety stand, were paying almost exclusive attention to his person.

As he swam along in the cooling green water, employing first his side stroke, then his breast stroke, and finally his strong back stroke, he thought he heard a voice calling to him a little bit in toward shore. He stopped swimming, looked, and indeed there was a person, a young man of about thirty with short brown hair, treading water not five feet away.

"Excuse me," the young man said, "aren't you Mr. Pontopolis?"

"Yes."

"Uh, can I speak to you alone?"

Cecil looked left and he looked right. There wasn't

a soul anywhere within fifty yards.

"Shoot," he said.

"I know you don't know me, Mr. Pontopolis, but I'm Steve Friend. I'm a lawyer in East Hampton, and I was a Democratic candidate for Village Councilman two years ago. I'm not sure if you're aware of this, Mr. Pontopolis, but there are very few Democrats in East Hampton, and as a result the Republicans always win and, frankly, they get away with murder, politically speaking."

"I didn't know that."

"Well, the reason I've come to see you, Mr. Pontopolis, is that I think the Republicans are getting away with murder with you. I think it is a crime that a private citizen should have to pay parking fines the way they are making you pay them, and I just wanted you to know that I'm going to do something about it."

"Like what?"

"I'm not sure. Perhaps there is a law, a MAXIMUM that a person can be fined for a parking ticket. Perhaps it is illegal to have an exclusive beach in the first place."

"Suppose I WANT to pay these fines."

Steve Friend looked at the billionaire in wonder.

"This is a matter of PRINCIPLE," he finally said. "There are others that this could happen to. We must think of the others."

And then he splashed a little, turned, and swam off.

*　　*　　*

That evening, at the regularly scheduled meeting of the Village Board, Mayor Breckinridge triumphantly announced that Mr. Pontopolis had gone swimming that day, and his fines now totalled $2,293,760. This was nearly halfway toward the total of four million dollars needed for the construction of the bypass. having considered this total, and having considered the fact that Mr. Pontopolis would most assuredly go swimming on Saturday, and probably on Sunday, since it was a weekend, and he had not missed even a week day as yet, the board had decided to go ahead with the plans to build the bypass, and also to begin work on the beach pavillion. And there would be more. After giving the matter some thought, the board had decided to fix all the potholes in all the roads in town, double the size of the police force, build on the Village Green a full scale replica of the way the town looked in 1670, and build at least half a dozen new parking lots. As for the suggestion that parkland be purchased, if and when Mr. Pontopolis' fines exceeded a hundred million dollars, the possibility of buying parkland would be fully investigated. It was, after all, the most expensive of all the proposals, with real estate prices being what they were and all.

The townspeople greeted this news with great enthusiasm and excitement, and they shouted a great cheer as, with each proposal, the board voted unanimously for its acceptance. By ten o'clock, when all the proposals were passed into law, and the meeting adjourned, hardly anyone noticed the slight summer drizzle that had begun to fall. The townspeople simply put their jackets over their heads and trotted out to their cars, parked on the street outside.

*   *   *

On Saturday, it rained steadily and nobody went to the beach. On Sunday it rained even harder, and on Monday it looked like the storm might develop into a hurricane. Mayor Breckinridge was very worried about all this. Here they had committed the Village to nearly ten million dollars worth of expenses, and Mr. Pontopolis's parking tickets were only bringing in two. Still, it couldn't rain forever.

94

Could it?

On Tuesday afternoon, Steve Friend ran from his car, through the rain, and into the East Hampton Village Hall. Taking his coat off in the lobby, he spotted the sign on the bulletin board, calling an emergency meeting of the Village Board on Wednesday night. It didn't surprise him. He probably would have done the same thing.

Steve threw his raincoat over his arm, walked briskly through the main lobby, up a flight of stairs, and into the musty records room of the Village. Records here went back nearly three hundred years. Steve stepped deftly around the metal bucket on the floor, catching the drip from the leak in the ceiling, and walked up to old man Addison, who was in charge of the records room, and sat at a big oak desk off in a corner. Addison got the books that Steve needed, because he legally couldn't refuse to do so. But in three days Addison had not said one word to Steve Friend, and he did not do so now.

"The Surveyor's Records, please. From 1760 — 1790."

Addison disappeared and returned. The records landed on the oak desk with a loud thump.

"Thank you very much," Steve Friend said.

Steve sat on a metal chair and opened the book out on a metal table. He'd been through most of it already. He worked at it, flipping through one page after another for almost an hour, when suddenly he found what he had been looking for. His heart pounding in his chest, he hastily copied down the information he needed in the small notebook he carried. Addison, across the room, was reading a copy of Hunting and Fishing magazine. He didn't even look up.

Wednesday morning, the sun rose bright and clear. It rose over the huge beachfront mansions in Southampton, their lawns sparkling with the morning dew. It rose over the windmills of East

Hampton, still damp from the three days of rain, and it rose over the seagulls, circling the beaches, both restricted and unrestricted, that were already stirring with beachgoers, carrying their blankets, chairs and towels for a full day by the sea.

At the back of one of these beaches, there stood the overweight figure of policeman Pat O'Flaherty, hands behind his back, and surprisingly confident that sometime this morning he would be giving out a parking ticket bearing a fine of $2,621,440. Ten o'clock came, then ten-thirty. At a quarter to eleven, eagle-eye O'Flaherty saw a car he had never seen before approaching the parking lot that he was so carefully supervising. It was a grey Plymouth, at least ten years old. It had a large dent in the left front fender and, worst of all, on none of the windows did it bear a parking sticker. O'Flaherty waddled over to the car as it came to a halt, and he already had out his ticket book, when the driver of the car got out and stared him right in the face. It was Mayor Breckinridge.

"And what do you think you're doing?" the Mayor asked.

"I'm giving this car a parking ticket," O'Flaherty answered.

"This is my WIFE'S car."

"Well, it doesn't hve a parking sticker."

"I just came down here to see you give Pontopolis his two million dollar parking ticket. My car is in the shop. It needs a new water pump."

"Well your WIFE'S car doesn't have a parking sticker."

"O'Flaherty, you KNOW I live in East Hampton Village. I'm the MAYOR, for gosh sakes."

"You should have got your wife a parking sticker," O'Flaherty said with finality.

O'Flaherty walked around to the back of the car and began writing down the license number in his parking book. He was committed. The Mayor stood there, leaning against his car and just glared at him.

"It's only five dollars," the policeman said.

Ten minutes went by, the ticket had long since been written and placed under the rusty windshield wiper, and neither man had said anything further to the other. Then, off in the distance, they both heard the unmistakable roar of the familiar handmade Ferrari sports car.

"That's HIM," the men said, almost in unison.

The little car appeared, heavily laden down with people and beach supplies. There were, in the front seats of the car, Cecil Pontopolis at the wheel, and Princess Adreanne in a white hat. Then, in the small jump seat in the back, there sat a second man whom O'Flaherty had never seen before.

The car parked, almost at the feet of the mayor and the policeman, and the three people got out, all dressed in their bathing suits for the beach.

"I'd like you to meet Mayor Breckinridge," O'Flaherty said. "He's the Mayor of East Hampton."

The Mayor held out his hand, and Cecil took it.

"This is Princess Adreanne von Hapsburg," Cecil said, "and this is my accountant, Jack Brady."

Everyone shook hands all around.

"I'm just out for the day," Brady said. "Thought I'd see if the town is as lovely as Cecil here says it is. It most certainly is."

Cecil walked around to the trunk of the little car to get out his magazines.

"Well," O'Flaherty said, "I guess we better get started. You haven't got a parking sticker so I'll have to give you a ticket.

"WAIT!" a stranger shouted.

Everyone turned to look at the slim, young man who seemed to have appeared out of a bush at the side of the parking lot.

"You can't give this man a ticket. He's a resident

97

of East Hampton Village and fully entitled to a parking sticker."

"Who the hell are you?" O'Flaherty asked.

"I'm Steve Friend, that's who the hell I am."

"He's that young whippersnapper who ran for office, trying to change everything in town," the Mayor said.

"Where's your car? Let me see your parking sticker," O'Flaherty said, sniffing this way and that.

"I don't have a car. I got dropped off. And you can't give this man any more tickets. Furthermore, all the tickets you already gave him are invalid. He's a resident of the Village."

"My property's not in the Village," Cecil said. "It's fifty feet OUTSIDE the Village. I saw the Village map."

"The map is wrong," Steve said. "I checked back in the Village records to 1782, when they originally laid out the Village. They measured the Village limits from the shoreline of Georgica Pond. The Pond had more water in it back then. It was bigger, and the shoreline was much closer to you. You're in the Village limits by at least fifteen feet. These documents prove it." Friend held up some papers he had copied.

"Let me see that," O'Flaherty said, walking over to have a look.

"I could choose NOT to get a parking sticker," Cecil said.

Friend handed the documents to O'Flaherty.

"Do you know what they are planning to do with this town? Have you any idea what they're going to do with your money? When they get done with it, you won't even recognize East Hampton. They're going to build a six-lane superhighway as a bypass; they're going to build hot dog stands and boardwalks on the dunes; they're going to. . ."

"Shut up," Mayor Breckinridge said.

"Is this true?" Cecil asked.

"Yes, it's true. Four million dollars is a lot of money."

Cecil Pontopolis looked at his stack of Saturday Evening Posts, then he looked at O'Flaherty, who was staring at him with his mouth open. Cecil made a decision.

"We'd like to get a parking sticker," he said simply.

*　　*　　*

Mayor Breckinridge stood in his office with his hands behind his back. In front of him, on his old oak desk, there were stacked about three hundred sheets of paper, the plans and reports for the expenditure of the anticipated four million dollars. Behind the Mayor, the door to the main lobby was ajar, and Mr. Breckinridge could hear the clerk at the window issuing Cecil Pontopolis his precious yellow parking sticker.

"Portuckolis?"

"No, Pontopolis."

"Would you spell that, please?"

"P as in Portofino, O as in Orleans, N as in Nice. . ."

The Mayor walked around his desk, over to the window, where the rusty old air conditioner was humming raggedly away. He took a step back, and with one swift motion, he kicked it. Immediately, the air conditioner made a different and much healthier sound. It was a happy hum. And then, as the Mayor stared down at it in astonishment, he heard the thermostat kick in, as it had never done before. It didn't seem possible, but the fact was that the air conditioner was once and finally, fixed.

Peacocks, Raccoons And Parrots

They've been having a lot of trouble with animals in Montauk lately. The other day a man opened his garage door to find a full grown peacock strutting around. And then just yesterday, I got a call from my father that a raccoon had disappeared inside his boat.

"I got a call from Carl Darenberg at the Marine Basin," he said. "They'd had a raccoon in the boathouse, they'd shooed him out, and he'd run down the dock and jumped aboard my boat."

Dad's boat is a twenty-eight foot inboard.

"He's hiding somewhere in the cabin. Everyone is afraid to get him out. No telling what damage he's done."

"Thing to do," I said, "is sink the boat. Raccoons can't swim well. That'll get him out."

"I don't know what we'd do without you," Dad said.

Later in the day, I heard an interesting story about a parrot. This couple was new to Montauk and they had three kids and they had this parrot. The parrot loved the husband and he loved the kids. The husband or the kids could take the parrot out of the cage and he'd fly around and land on people's arms, coo in their ears, rub against their cheeks.

But when the wife was home, you had to keep the parrot in his cage. The parrot hated the wife. If the wife came near the cage the parrot would shriek menacingly and try to bite her. The wife couldn't even kiss her husband in front of him because the parrot would go berserk with rage and try to break out of his cage. God knows why they ever kept the parrot.

One day, though, with the wife in town shopping, the husband and the kids took the parrot out and let him fly around the living room. A window had been left open, however, and out flew the parrot over toward the house next door. Everybody ran out to see the parrot fly into the neighbor's garage. Nobody was around. And so the father went inside and found the parrot under the neighbor's car.

"Here Polly, here Polly," the husband coaxed.

But the parrot would not budge.

One hour later, the wife came home.

"Come next door," the husband said. "You can coax the parrot out. Polly hates you."

Down on her hands and knees, the wife glared under the car at the parrot. The parrot glared back. But he would not come out.

"I have a brilliant idea," he said. He too got down on his hands and knees. "Kiss me."

And so, there on the concrete floor of the neighbor's garage, the new couple kissed. And at that moment, the neighbor's wife walked into her garage, car keys in hand.

"Good afternoon," the husband said. "We were just trying to get our parrot."

The neighbor's wife fled.

The Reindeer Who Couldn't Fly

When my grandfather was a boy, he says, he would lean out the window of his bedroom late on Christmas eve, and listen to Santa's sleigh and reindeer as they made their way across the dark December nighttime sky. There would be sleighbells, and there would be the crack of Santa's whip, and then, clear and strong, the voice of Santa himself shouting out the names of the reindeer.

"On Alphonse, on Heathcliffe, on Melvin, on Egbert. On Bananas, on Pickles, on Clarence, on Herbert. To the top of the wall. Come, dash away, dash away, dash away all."

"What?" I wanted to know. "On Alphonse? On Heathcliffe? Those aren't the names of the reindeer."

"They aren't now," my grandfather would say, arching a brow. "But they certainly were then. They would ride across the nighttime sky and Santa would clearly call out their names as they went. That was them."

"But what happened?"

"Well, THAT, my grandson, is a long, long story," my grandfather continued. "But if you'd like to hear it, you can pull up a pillow and sit here by the fire."

And with that, grandfather reached over, struck a match, and lit his favorite pipe.

* * *

I was nine years old at the time. I was a little small for my age, but I was a good woodsman, and I used to thoroughly enjoy walking to school through the forest. Our house was on Daniel's Hole Road, you know, and the East Hampton school to which I went was over a mile away. There were no school buses when I was a boy, and so we walked, my friend Ed and I, down a narrow winding path, from Daniel's Hole Road to the East Hampton School on Newtown Lane.

Well, that winter when I was nine years old, was one of the coldest I ever remember. It wasn't even Thanksgiving when we had our first snowfall. And by the first week in December, there was nearly three feet of snow on the ground. We laced up high boots, and wore heavy coats, and we trudged down the path through the woods to the school. It took an hour or more.

The day I want to talk about was a Friday, about two weeks before Christmas, and it was cold and crisp, like most of the others we had that very cold year. At ten after three, the school bell clanged and Mrs. Barnaby dismissed us for the day. We all got our books and tucked them under our arms. And Eddie and I put on our heavy woolen coats, and headed out down the snow-covered trail toward home.

Now, it gets dark pretty early that time of year, and we'd only been walking for about three quarters of an hour when the sun set and night settled in on the woods between school and Daniel's Hole Road.

"What's that?" Eddie asked.

I peered through the darkness. And through the branches of some snow covered trees, I saw some men with lanterns.

"Let's go look," Eddie said.

"No. I'm scared."

There must have been a hundred men with lanterns there in this clearing over on the other side of the trees. In spite of myself, I followed Eddie close behind, sneaking as quietly as I could, trying not to let any of the men there see me. We crunched softly through the snow, and when we had gotten quite near, we crouched down behind a fallen log. We were so close, we could see everything that was going on. But no one could see us.

What a sight it was. At one end of this clearing, there was a small shack with a pot-bellied stove inside and a dozen men standing about. There was a sign over the door, and I will never forget what the sign said.

It said, "THE REINDEER FLYING SCHOOL."

The clearing itself extended for almost a quarter of a mile, and if I'd known then what I know now, I'd have guessed that this was a flier's runway. But you know, there were no airplanes back then. And I think it is only a coincidence that today the East Hampton Airport is located on the very site where Eddie and I saw this clearing way back then.

Lanterns had been placed on each side of this clearing, and as the sky slowly grew darker, the lanterns flickered and glowed with an increasingly bright intensity. The men, meanwhile, trudged about.

"How much longer?" one of them shouted.

"Any minute," another shouted back.

"Keep those horses away."

"They're way back. Don't want to scare them. Have we got the hot cider?"

"In the shack. Mary's heating it up."

This was, indeed, one of the strangest conversations I had ever heard. I looked at Eddie, and he looked at me. It was obvious that he couldn't make head or tails of it either.

And then, one of the men pointed a mittened

finger straight up at the sky.

"Look! Here he comes!"

Both Eddie and I looked up. And would you believe it, there, racing across the sky, was Santa and his sleigh and eight tiny reindeer. They were silhouetted clearly against the bright moon, and as they circled, coming lower and lower, I could hear the panting of the reindeers' breath, and the crack of the whip, and the call of Mr. Claus from his perch at the front of the sleigh.

"On Alphonse, on Heathcliff, on Melvin, on Egbert. On Bananas, on Pickles, on Clarence, on Herbert."

Eddie turned to me.

"Christmas isn't for two more weeks," he whispered. "What is going on?"

"I don't know," I said.

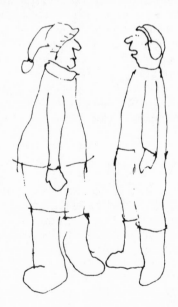

Santa circled lower and lower. And then, as some of the men stood down at the end of the runway and waved lanterns over their heads, Santa came in for a landing. It was one of the most exciting things that I have ever seen. The lead reindeer touched down, then the second reindeer, then the third. Finally the sleigh itself set down, and as the runners from the sleigh hissed across the snow, a cloud of white snowflakes billowed into the air, shimmering in the lanternlight.

The reindeer and the sleigh slowed down, then came to a stop just in front of the small wooden shack. And all these men, whooping and hollering, came running out of the shack to greet the big man in the red and white snowsuit.

"Mr. Claus. Mr. Claus. How are you? It's so good to see you."

Santa stood up in his sleigh and raised his arms.

"Thank you, thank you," he said. "It's been a long flight. But it's been an enjoyable one. I'm so glad to be here."

And once again, everyone commenced whooping and hollering as they had done before.

Then Santa Claus hopped down from his sleigh and brushed the snow off his suit. He walked around to the back of his sleigh, and patted the outside of a very large white sack.

"Okay, everybody, we're here," he said.

He pulled on a very big red ribbon, the sack opened, and down jumped eight of the cutest little reindeer you have ever seen. There were now sixteen reindeer on the runway, eight big ones at the front of the sleigh, and eight frisky little ones, each about four feet high. I stood up.

"Get down," Eddie whispered.

And he pulled me by the coat, and I sat back down behind the log. Nobody had seen me.

"Okay, you little reindeer, line up," Santa said.

The eight little reindeer lined up all in a row, wagging their tails.

"Now listen carefully," Santa said to his reindeer. "Each of you will walk over to the Reindeer Flying School, have a sip of Mrs. Parsons' magic hot cider, then come on back here to the clearing."

The little reindeer were absolutely wide eyed.

"When you get back," Santa continued, "Mr.

Parsons himself will coach you in learning how to fly. Isn't that right, Mr. Parsons?"

"That's right," said a very tall man with white hair and a moustache.

"Are there any questions?" Santa asked.

"I'm scared," squeaked the smallest of the reindeer, a little tan one on the end.

"Oh, Blitzen, don't be scared. The older reindeer did this, didn't you, older reindeer?"

And the older reindeer, at the front of the sleigh, all stamped their feet and nodded.

"There, you see? Now. Single file. Just head right over to the flying school and have a sip of cider."

One by one, the eight tiny reindeer trotted off toward the little wooden shack at the end of the clearing.

"I don't believe this," Eddie whispered.

"I don't either," I said. "But it's happening."

Santa walked back over to his sleigh, reached in, and pulled out a big stack of red blankets. Then he threw them, one at a time, over the backs of the eight big reindeer.

"Just rest," he said. "Cool off and relax. We'll be leaving to go back to the North Pole within the hour."

Mr. Parsons came over.

"How is everything at the North Pole?" he asked.

"Just fine. Making presents like crazy."

"Anything new this year?"

"Oh, the elves have got a few surprises up their sleeves. Just like they always do. But you know my big concern is these eight tiny reindeer. I hope you can get them to fly. These older reindeer have reached their mandatory retirement age. So, if the young reindeer can't fly, I don't know what I'll do. Just skip Christmas, I guess."

"Don't even give it a second thought," Mr. Parsons said. "Mary's magic cider worked the last time, didn't it?"

"Yes, it did."

"And this time we've got something entirely new. Harry?"

Mr. Parsons turned and held out his hand to one of the men standing nearby. The man handed Mr. Parsons a rolled up piece of paper.

"This, Mr. Santa Claus, is a Certificate of Graduation."

Mr. Parsons unrolled the paper.

"Each of your eight tiny reindeer will be given a certificate, just like this, complete with this red seal and ribbon down here in the corner."

"Wow," Santa Claus said.

"We think of everything."

At that moment, the first of the eight tiny reindeer emerged from the shack. He trotted gingerly back toward Santa Claus and the sleigh, then stopped next to Mr. Parsons, wagging his little tail.

"This is Dasher," Santa Claus said.

"Howdy do, Dasher," Mr. Parsons said, patting him between the antlers. "Now everybody, get to your places, and Dasher is about to learn to fly."

All the workmen, and as I said, there must have been a hundred of them there in the clearing, ran down the runway and bent down to work on the lanterns. Some lanterns had gone out and had to be

relit. Others had to be made brighter or softer.

"Let's go, Dasher! Come on, boy!"

And Mr. Parsons, with one hand on the reindeer's antlers, broke into a trot. Dasher kicked up his heels, and then galloped alongside, all the time listening to the soft words Mr. Parsons said. They ran down the field about halfway, and then, all of a sudden, the reindeer was off the ground. Mr. Parsons gave it a mittened slap on the behind, and off it went, up into the sky.

"Atta way, Dasher," Santa Claus shouted, jumping up and down.

Dasher dove crazily off to one side, pulled up, then glided over the clearing, pawing at the air with his hooves. He had the most amazed expression on his face.

"Settle down, settle down," Mr. Parsons shouted, running along underneath. "You've got it."

111

Dasher flew off to the south, then off to the north, then finally returned to the clearing and came roaring in for a landing at breakneck speed. He slipped in the snow, tumbled head over heels and slid to a halt on his belly right in front of Mr. Claus.

"Not bad, not bad," Mr. Parsons said, running over. "Just a little overeager."

Dasher shook himself, and snow flew all over everybody. "Well, anyway," Mr. Parsons said. "Here is your Certificate of Graduation. You've earned it." And he took out the rolled up piece of paper and tied it with a ribbon around the little reindeer's neck.

"Next," he said.

* * *

It was the most remarkable thing I have ever seen. Next Dancer flew. Then Prancer and Vixen. Then Comet and Cupid and Donner and, well, then there was Blitzen.

Blitzen and Mr. Parsons came back from the far end of the clearing together, all discouraged and all out of breath.

"I can't do it," Blitzen said.

"Yes, you can. Yes, you can. Let's try again."

And so, off they ran, Mr. Parsons with his hands on Blitzen's antlers, down the runway a second time until they were out of sight.

"I hope he makes it," Santa Claus said. "We can't fly with just seven reindeer."

But Mr. Parsons came walking back with Blitzen, puffing even harder.

"I don't understand it," he said. "You did drink Mary's magic cider, didn't you?"

"Of course, I did. But I'm scared."

"Now don't be scared. Turn around. Just one more time."

"You can do it, Blitzen," Santa shouted.

"Again, they ran down the runway, stomping through the snow until they were out of sight. And again, they walked back, more bedraggled than they had ever been before.

"I've got to sit down," Mr. Parsons puffed. "Boy, this is tiring. Come with me, Santa. Let's go inside the shack for a minute. Don't worry. He'll get it."

"I sure hope so," Santa Claus said.

Santa put his arm around Mr. Parsons and helped him off in the direction of the shack. They disappeared inside, and the wooden door banged behind them.

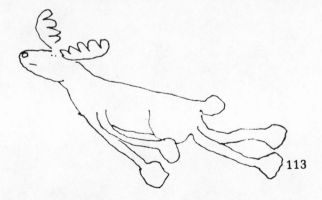

113

And that's when I got up.

"What are you doing?" Eddie whispered.

"Don't worry. I have a plan. I'll see you home."

In the darkness, lit only by the lanternlight, nobody really noticed me walking over to Blitzen. This little reindeer was just pacing around, pawing at the snow, and sobbing little sobs.

"Hello, Mr. Blitzen."

The little reindeer looked up. "Huh?" he asked.

"Mr. Blitzen, would you help me?" I had on my saddest face. "Mr. Blitzen, I'm just a nine-year-old boy, and I live in these parts, and I've lost my way in the woods. Could you take me home?"

"Take you home?" Blitzen asked. "How could I take you home?"

"You could fly me home," I said. "You see, if you could fly me up in the sky, I'm sure I could look down

and see my house. I know I could. And then I wouldn't be lost. You could fly down and just leave me off right in my yard."

"But I can't fly," Blitzen said.

"Of course you can fly. All the reindeer can fly. I've seen them."

And with that, I climbed on the little reindeer's back.

"Giddyap."

The reindeer turned and looked me right in the eye.

"Giddyap?" he said.

"Isn't that what I say?" I said. "Giddyap is what I say to horses to make them go. It should make you go, too."

"Well, then giddyap it is," Blitzen said.

And with that, the little reindeer charged down the runway once again, taking long bounding strides through the snow. The lanterns flashed by, and I hung onto Blitzen's antlers as best I could. And then, as the cold night wind stung my cheeks, I found myself up in the air, skimming over the trees and the clouds.

"You're flying!" I shouted.

"Well, of course," Blitzen replied. "I'll get you home."

Down below, I could see the twinkling lights of Sag Harbor and the flashing beacon of the Montauk Lighthouse. We flew past Southampton, made a big wide circle over Westhampton, and came in low across the Shinnecock Canal.

"Do you see your house?" Blitzen asked.

"Wait! There it is."

Sure enough, right where I knew it was all along, I saw our little house with the big front lawn. White smoke was curling from the chimney.

"You can land right on the lawn," I said, "but be careful." I remembered some of the landings I'd seen.

Blitzen came in slowly and carefully and made the most gentle landing that any reindeer had made all night, right there on my front lawn.

"Thank YOU," Blitzen said. And he gave me this great big wet lick on the face. Then he was gone.

*　　*　　*

"Are you sure this all really happened?" I asked my grandfather.

Grandfather paused for a moment to relight his pipe.

"Well, Eddie remembered it," he said. He looked at me and cocked an eyebrow again. "At least, Eddie saw me going down the clearing, and he didn't see me again until the following morning. But you know what the real proof of all that was?"

"What?" I asked.

"Well, on Christmas morning, I went downstairs and there, along with all the toys that were under my Christmas tree, was a special Certificate of Appreciation from the Reindeer Flying School. Old Blitzen had gone back, and he had told Mr. Parsons about all I had done. And Mr. Parsons had made up this special certificate just for me. Now what do you think of that?"

I thought for a minute.

"Where is it? Do you still have it?"

Grandfather took another long puff on his pipe.

"You know," he said. "A number of years ago, I think I gave that certificate to your father."

Justice in Southampton Traffic Court

The room is perhaps typical of all small-town courtrooms. It has an American flag in one corner, with a no smoking sign not far away. There is an air conditioner, a large white and black wall clock with a second hand, two exit signs, a lineoleum floor and a large calendar, courtesy of the Queens Industrial Electric Company. Along one wall, facing out to the street, are a row of windows covered with venetian blinds. The blinds are clean, and they are in the down position. They are open, however, and you can see out to the street just six feet away where the shoppers walk mechanically back and forth carrying their merchandise to their cars. The shoppers could look in if they wanted to, although they'd have to get embarrassingly close for the courtroom to make sense through the blinds. There, just a dozen steps from the shopping street, Hampton Road, the law and order of the township is maintained, with this person being sent off to jail, that person given a warning of one sort or another, the other person being acquitted for lack of evidence. There is, perhaps, just one unusual thing about this courtroom. And that particular Saturday morning, the thirty or so persons waiting inside, waiting for the judge to appear at ten A.M., are consciously aware of it. The courtroom, it seems, is really only a temporary building. It is one-story high, and it has a very low ceiling, and it was brought in in one piece by a large trailer twelve years earlier when Town Hall next door became so overcrowded. The courtroom building actually sits on large cinderblocks, and you have the feeling that if you jumped up and down, which you won't do because it is indeed a courtroom, you could probably make it move or fall off its foundations. Justice, in Southampton, then, was hauled in by a truck. Someday, when the people decide it is no longer doing its job, justice could be packed up in one afternoon and taken away.

At exactly the stroke of ten, the procession of court clerk, sergeant-at-arms and judge in flowing robes, makes its way up the corridor between the folding chairs, toward the judge's bench at the head of the room. No one stands up as the judge enters the room, as they do on a usual court day. This is Saturday morning traffic court, and the entire courtroom is filled with people accused of some minor violation, usually written out on a yellow traffic ticket clutched in the left or right hand. The people are, by definition, angry, or feeling guilty, or impatient, having been given a ticket for something they didn't do or did do. (The ticket reads YOU ARE ORDERED TO APPEAR...) For the most part, they are young men with slicked-back hair, school or leather jackets and jeans. They aren't going to stand up unless they have to.

The sergeant-at-arms, a Southampton Town policeman, places himself at one corner of the room and stands facing the judge and the accused. He takes off his police hat to reveal a bald head. On his right hip, he has a gun. Presumably, he will shoot anybody who goes berserk or wants to violently object to whatever the justice is that is being meted out.

119

The court clerk, a very pretty blonde girl with a blue sweater, pearls and a pink ribbon in her hair, seats herself in back of the bench. She shuffles the papers indicating the various offenses, looking for the first one to hand to the judge. Throughout the proceedings, she keeps her lips pursed and tight in an attitude of moral indignation. She seems to find it hard to believe that so many people could have done so many wrong things in just one week in the Town of Southampton. Certainly, SHE is not about to forgive any of them.

There is silence.

"James J. Abbott?" the judge calls, peering out through his thick glasses, looking this way and that.

A young man with a SOUTHAMPTON COLLEGE jacket gets up and walks to the bench, or rather, saunters up to the bench. On arrival, he plants both feet on the floor about two feet apart, clasps his hands behind his back and lowers his head. A modified position of the military At Ease.

The judge is Edwin Berkery, according to the nameplate, and he has huge, giant eyes magnified behind his thick glasses. He is a large, dignified man otherwise, with a thick head of bushy white hair and a broad mouth.

Now, after pronouncing the name "James J. Abbott" in slow broad monotones, he begins to speak at two hundred words a minute. He speaks like a phonograph record speeded up, an almost unintelligible paragraph of speech he is duty-bound to speak to every person that appears before him.

"James J. Abbott, you are CHARGED with violation of one-two-two-six of vehicle traffic law of the STATE of New York traveling sixty miles per hour in a fifty-mile-an-hour zone James J. Abbott the LAW requires that I ADVISE you of your right to a

COUNSEL at any stage of these proCEEDings do you WISH to get counsel THEN at some TIME and place where you and your counsel can be heard do you WANT to get a COUNSEL do you want an atTORney?"

James J. Abbott, age approximately twenty, looks at the judge blankly.

"Do you want an attorney?" the judge repeats, but slower.

"No, I don't want an attorney."

"How do you plead?"

"Guilty, your honor."

The accused speaks softly, and the judge speaks softly, but in the silence of this courtroom, everything can be heard. Everyone wants to find out what to say to this judge to get the smallest sentence, or to get off. What kind of a judge is this man? How he is feeling? What did he eat for breakfast?

The proceedings move rapidly, almost like a treadmill. The fines are meted out. Fifteen dollars. Twenty-five dollars. Twenty dollars. Case dismissed. As the judge listens to one accused, the previous accused is standing alongside, pulling his wallet out to pay his fine to the pretty clerk of the court. The sergeant-at-arms stands alongside with his gun at his side.

"Joyce Adamski step up to the bench."

A tall, thin man walks up to the bench. He wears a leather jacket and has leather gloves sticking out of his back pants pocket. The judge looks at him closely through his thick glasses.

"You're not Joyce Adamski," he says.

"Uh, no I'm not," the man says.

* * *

The judge deals with a young man who has been charged with speeding. The speeding, it turns out, was to take his wife to the hospital. And the officer writing the ticket said the only reason he wrote the ticket was that he caught him on radar, and so he HAD to write one. Bring a letter from the doctor and show it to the judge and he'll dismiss it, the policeman said.

The judge looks at the doctor's letter.

"Case dismissed."

And then, wishing to appear as a regular fellow, he breaks out of his routine to ask a question.

"How's your wife?"

"Not good, not good. The doctor says she's got a nervous problem. Twenty-nine years old she is, and she acts like forty. You wouldn't believe it. I don't know what we're going to do with all the doctor's bills. You know what they're charging these days at the Southampton Hospital?"

The judge looks at the clerk for help. He's still got plenty of cases to go.

* * *

"Thomas Cotton step up to the bench."

"Thomas Cotton, you are CHARGED with violation of one-three-eight-seven of vehicle traffic law of the STATE of New York going through a stop sign Thomas Cotton the LAW requires that I ADVISE you of your right to a COUNSEL at any stage of these proCEEDings so you wish to get a counsel THEN at some TIME and place where you and your counsel can be heard do you WANT to get a COUNSEL do you want an atTORney?"

Silence. Perhaps he hadn't heard.

"Do you want an attorney?"

Still silence.

"How do you plead?"

Silence.

"Do you plead guilty? Do you plead not guilty?"

The man shifts from one foot to the other, but says nothing.

"If you plead guilty, we'll settle it here and now. If you plead not guilty, we'll set a date for a trial."

Silence.

"Come on man! Guilty or not guilty!"

Silence. The sergeant-at-arms stiffens, moves his hand slightly toward his gun.

"Look, we haven't got all day. Did you do it or didn't you? How do you plead?"

More silence.

"Well, I'll just put you down as not guilty, and we'll set a trial date. How's that?"

It suddenly occurs to the judge what is happening in front of him.

"What is your name?" he asks. "Where do you live? Tell me, where do you live?"

There is still silence.

"Go back to your seat, and I'll call you later. Go out and splash some water on your face."

The man turns and walks out of the courtroom. Later, he is called again and apologizes profusely.

The judge fines him fifteen dollars.

*   *   *

Throughout the proceedings, a tall black man with a full beard has been sitting on the end seat in the front row. He is probably the dirtiest person in the room, covered from head to foot with dirt from the potato fields. He is a migrant worker. He wears a torn shirt, torn shoes and blue jean overalls, which contain two earmarked paperbacks in the back pockets and what appears to be a flashlight in the front pocket. Occasionally he takes out one of his paperback books and refers to it. It is a pocket dictionary.

"Lindsey B. Lacey, step up."

123

The black man gets up and a 45-rpm record drops to the floor. He places it on his seat. A white girl of about twenty sitting next to him also gets up, and the two of them walk to the bench.

"Lindsey B. Lacey?"

"This is him, your honor," the girl says.

"Who are you?"

"I'm Susan Wasserman from Southampton. I'm a volunteer with the Eastern Farm Workers Association. Mr. Lacey here doesn't speak, and I'm representing him."

"He's mute?"

"Yes."

"But he understands?"

"Yes, he does."

"Mr. Lacey is charged with theft of services," the judge says, proceeding to launch on the long monologue he is required to say to everybody.

"It says here he's accused of theft of services," the judge repeats when he is done.

"He ate a meal in the restaurant at Grants," Sue Wasserman says. "He didn't have enough money to pay for it. He was twenty-five cents short. But he's offering to pay for it here and now, and hopes this will settle things. He's already spent a night in jail."

Judge Berkery blinks for a moment.

"Is the manager here? The manager who placed the charges?"

The manager, actually a young assistant manager in a maroon suede coat, walks quickly to the bench.

"Now this man is offering to pay for his meal," the judge says. "Is that all right with you?"

"Well, it's more complicated than that," the manager says. "You see, he comes into the store almost every day. He comes in at two, three in the

124

afternoon, and he stays right up until eleven. He never buys anything. He's just hanging around. We've asked him to leave, and he won't leave."

"Well, I can't do anything about THAT," the judge says.

"Yesterday, he came in with a 45 record, and he went back to the record department and wanted them to play it for him. So then, last night, when he couldn't pay for his meal, we had him arrested."

"Well, now, he's offering to PAY for his meal. You want to drop the charges?"

The assistant manager moves from one foot to the other. He doesn't say anything.

"You want me to issue you an INJUNCTION to keep this man out of your store," the judge says. "But I can't do that. The court isn't empowered to do anything like that." The judge turns to Ms. Wasserman. "Look, they don't want this man in their store. He's a nuisance. You've heard how it is. Can you tell him to stay out of there?"

"I can try. I'll TRY to keep him from going in there."

"She'll TRY to keep him out of there," the judge says to the assistant manager. "There are no guarantees."

"He lives next door to the store," Susan Wasserman says. "He lives in the camp there, and it's pretty run down. He just wanders into the store."

The assistant manager agrees to drop the charges, and the judge produces two forms, one for the assistant manager to sign and one for the farm worker to sign. The farm worker is given a pen, and, very slowly and very carefully, he leans over the paper and begins to read.

"That's a release, is all," the judge says. "It just

says they are dropping the charges."

"He's still reading," Sue Wasserman says.

The second hand on the wall clock turns. Five minutes go by in silence. Eight. Ten. Lindsey B. Lacey is still reading. Very slowly.

"You tell your client to stay out of that store," the judge says to Sue Wasserman. "If he's brought into this court again, I'll be much harder on him. I'll send him to Riverhead, you understand? Jail."

"I understand."

The judge turns to the assistant manager.

"And you understand he's got to be breaking a law before you bring him in here. You can't just have an injunction to keep a man out of your store."

Lindsey Lacey is still reading. Sue Wasserman opens her suede shoulder bag and begins to fish around inside for the money to pay for the meal that Linsey Lacey ate. She finds a metal Band-Aid collection box, opens it and withdraws several coins and dollars. The assistant manager is touched by this.

"Forget it," he says. "The meal is on us."

Finally, Lindsey Lacey finishes his reading and, very slowly, signs the release that he will not be bringing charges against the multi-million dollar Grant City Department Store for having him arrested.

* * *

The last case of the day brings a very well-dressed gray-haired man before the bench. He wears a business suit and a heavy suede coat with a fur collar.

"It says here you are charged with driving an unregistered motor scooter," the judge says.

"Yes. It's twelve years old, and it's been in the repair shop for the last five months. I just got it out and was trying it out. My secretary told me the registration was in order. But it apparently wasn't. It had expired while in repair. The very next day I went out and got a new registration. You can see the dates."

The man set the registration in front of the judge.

"So here's the registration," the judge said.

"Yes."

"Case dismissed," the judge said. "And thank you for coming."

Nice Work

Every few days, this newspaper gets inquiries from people about our advertising rates. When the inquiries come from the immediate area, we dispatch a salesman to take care of it. But when the inquiry comes from New York City or Chicago or Los Angeles, we resort to the mails. We will send out a manila envelope filled with rate sheets, copies of the paper and testimonials, and then, a week later follow up this mailing with a telephone call.

Up until last year, this method served us quite well. But beginning last year, we discovered that an alarming number of people who inquire about advertising never receive our manila envelope.

"Nothing's arrived?"

"Not a thing."

"Gee, we mailed that to you almost ten days ago."

A careful study of this situation has revealed that of every ten envelopes we send out, we can count on no more than seven actually arriving. This compares dismally to years gone by when it used to be ten out of ten.

It is interesting to note that until last year the Postal Service operated almost entirely in a sea of red ink. Revenues were inadequate, costs were too high, and it was almost an annual crisis to see if enough government subsidies could be arranged to keep the operation going.

But then, just last month, the head of the Postal Service proudly announced in all the newspapers that the Post Office, for the first time ever, would be operating in the black. Revenues would exceed expenses at long last, and the Postal Service would actually declare a modest surplus at the end of this fiscal year.

People may wonder what sort of miracles the head of the Postal Service has wrought to bring about this wonderful state of affairs. I can only say that, to judge by our own personal experience with the mails, the achievement of a surplus has been accomplished in a very simple manner; the post office actually only mails a certain percentage of the letters they are given. The rest of the letters, all paid for with the stamps attached to the corners, are thrown away. And the money paid in is pure profit.

Let me give you an example of how this might work in the private sector. At a restaurant, for instance, four people order dinners. Ten minutes later, three dinners arrive, together with the check for all four.

Of course, you would say, the diners could simply not pay for the fourth dinner they never received, and this is true. But with the Postal Service, you have to pay BEFORE they do the work. So when they don't deliver your mail, you are in the position of complaining about it but having already been relieved of your money.

Two years ago, this newspaper did a story about the old-fashioned wooden post office in Wainscott. This wooden post office was being phased out, and a new, modern brick one was being built to take its place. The main reason for this, according to the postal authority, was the possibility of fire. All wooden post offices all over the country were being phased out wherever possible to be replaced by fireproof buildings. Postal trucks were being built as fireproof as possible too, and the great concern seemed to be that a day's pile of mail might actually be consumed in a fire.

Personally, I never thought that the postal service had to be so concerned about the safe storage of our letters. If something burned up in a fire, well, c'est la vie. You mail your letters and you take your chances. Wht seemed more important to me was the actual DELIVERY of the mail to the party for whom it was intended. On the other hand, if the Postal Service wants to make a profit, I guess there will just have to be some letters that go by the wayside.

* * *

Speaking of government inanities reminds me that just last week the Congress of the United States voted to continue spending more money than it takes in. A bill had been put forth in the House of Representatives which stated that government spending must not exceed government revenues in any fiscal year, and it was voted down.

The government has a very interesting double standard about money. For you and me, as private citizens in these United States, they say we can only spend what we take in. If we fall behind in any one year, and we can't pay our taxes, for example, they come in and they seize your property. Even a bankruptcy proceedings will not prevent the government from doing that.

For themselves, however, they allow that, year after year, they can spend more than they receive. They've been doing this for almost fifty years. What they get when they do this is called a "deficit," and every year the Congress votes to make it legal to increase what they call the "national debt."

Furthermore, the government never runs out of money when they run these "deficits," as ordinary citizens might. Every year, when it becomes apparent that there won't be enough dollars coming in to pay for their purchases, the government simply goes down to the basement in the Treasury Department and prints some more.

Could the government arrest itself for counterfeiting?

130

Wednesday Afternoon

At eleven o'clock of an April morning, I sat alone in the living room of one of those giant twenty-room summer "cottages" that line the beaches in Southampton. It was a sunny day. And outside, across the dunes just a few hundred feet away, the surf rumbled in against the beach, creating a roaring sound that rattled around inside those huge, wooden rooms.

There was a dining room off one side of this giant living room, and a sun porch over on the other. Everywhere there was creaky furniture made of wicker — a testimony of the power of humidity and mildew.

What to do? I wandered around and looked at the paintings on the walls for awhile. Gilt framed paintings they were, original oils, of young women dressed in the fashion at the turn of the century. Each as beautiful as the other, they stared dewy-eyed out into the room, frozen in time in the prime of their lives. Now they were old or gone. The thought depressed me.

There was wood near the fireplace, and had I been a little bolder, I would have bent down and stacked it up behind the grating to make a fire. There was a chill in the room. And, as at most of these old summer houses, there was inadequate heat. You weren't supposed to be in these places until the beginning of July. Before then, you were roughing it.

A half hour had gone now. It would be awhile before my hosts would return, and we would have lunch. I would wait.

And then I saw the book. The only book in the entire room. It lay on its side on an otherwise empty bookshelf at the far end of the living room, right next to the glass doors that led into the sun parlour. I walked over and picked it up.

READER'S DIGEST, SEPTEMBER 1967.

On the back, there was a painting of a western scene. Half a dozen people sat astride a split rail fence, watching a cowpuncher ride a bucking bronco in the middle of a ring. Across the way, an American flag waved from atop a white flag pole, and a yellow sun blazed from a pale green sky. Everyone looked very happy.

46TH YEAR: OVER 28 MILLION COPIES BOUGHT MONTHLY IN 14 LANGUAGES.

I sat down in one of the creaky wicker chairs and opened this volume of the Reader's Digest. Perhaps I would learn something.

MARTIN LUTHER KING'S TRAGIC DECISION, by Carl T. Rowan.

A tragic decision? Getting assassinated was a tragic decision? No. That isn't right. This was September 1967, and King was not yet dead. The magazine headline writer had to be referring to something else about King. I read the first few paragraphs.

"On a crisp, clear evening last April 4, the Rev. Martin Luther King stood in New York City's Riverside Church and delivered the most scathing denunciation of United States involvement in Vietnam ever made by so prominent an American. He labeled the United States 'the greatest purveyor of violence in the world today' and accused it of 'cruel manipulation of the poor.' He said the people of Vietnam 'watch as we poison their water, as we kill a million acres of their crops.'

"He stated that U.S. troops 'may have killed a million South Vietnamese — mostly children.' He

132

said that 'American soldiers test out our latest weapons' on the peasants of South Vietnam 'just as the Germans tested out new medicine and new tortures in the concentration camps of Europe.' He accused President Johnson of lying about peace overtures from Hanoi, and urged Americans to become 'conscientious objectors.'

"Reaction across the nation and around the world was immediate and explosive. Radios Moscow and Peking picked up King's words and spread them to distant capitals. In the White House, a Presidential aide shouted, 'My God, King has given a speech on Vietnam that goes right down the commie line!' "

"Civil rights leaders wrung their hands and began to plan steps to take the already splintered movement for Negro equality out from under the onus of King's broadside..."

The article went on and on in this manner. King was most certainly not going to be let off easy by the Reader's Digest or by anybody else. Roy Wilkins was brought in as opposed to Martin Luther King. Nobel Prize winner Ralph Bunche was quoted. Even Senator Edward Brooke disagreed publicly with King.

"Why did King reject the advice of his old civil rights colleagues?" the magazine continued. "Some say it was a matter of ego — that he was convinced that since he was the most influential Negro in the United States, President Johnson would HAVE to listen to HIM and alter U.S. policy in Vietnam. Others revived a more sinister speculation that had been whispered around Capitol Hill and in the nation's newsrooms for more than two years — talk of communists influencing the actions and words of the young minister."

I flipped through some other pages of this

twelve year-old magazine. Perhaps enlightenment lay elsewhere in the publication.

In the back of the magazine was a condensed book entitled UP FRONT IN VIETNAM, which I decided not to read. Instead, I decided to read TOMORROW'S AIRPORTS VS. THE GROUND BARRIER, which began on page 123.

"More terminal buildings and more concrete for runways are only parts of the solution," the article stated. "It will be an expensive undertaking, for which more than $2.5 billions are already committed to be spent before 1972."

The article went on to reassure me that in 1969 the 500-passenger Boeing 747 "jumbo" jet would be in operation, and "by 1975 there will be the U.S. Supersonic, a plane as long as a football field."

Where was everybody? When were they coming back for lunch anyway? Across the room, on a large marble pedestal, stood a rectangular bronze and glass wind-up clock. It said one o'clock. I got up and walked over to see if it was working. It wasn't. I returned to my chair.

HOW CALIFORNIA IS LICKING DRUG ADDICTION was an article I decided not to read. Drug addition was worse than ever.

And then there was the article on pornography in Cincinnati.

"...Following the verdict, Judge John W. Keefe sentenced Polly King to two consecutive terms of one to seven years in the state reformatory for women and fined her $4,000. In imposing sentence, Judge Keefe declared 'Mrs. King, the selling of obscenity is a filthy business for a man, but it is unbelievably vile for a woman.' "

My eyes were closing, and I was getting very tired. When was everyone coming home?

"The victory of the people of Cincinnati in the

King case stands as proof that concerned citizens in any community CAN lick the purveyors of newsstand obscenity — if they move with intelligence and determination..."

I put the magazine over my face to shut it up. Why the hell had it been the only thing in the room. As I dozed off, I remember reading one final sentence: "For information on reprints of these articles, see page 12."

Me Vs. Atari

The other day a game called Atari arrived at the house. I opened up the box and inside found a small electronic device with instructions for hooking it up to the television set. There was an electrical hookup, a main unit, and then two control sticks for each of two players to enjoy the game.

I tried the Atari game first with my daughter Maya, who is six. She held one control stick, I held the other, and we turned the TV set and the Atari game on to see what would happen. After awhile the set warmed up and we saw two paddles and a ball very clearly on the screen.

"Move the paddle, Daddy," my daughter said.

Sure enough, by moving the control stick around one side and another, I could make the paddle on the TV set move back and forth to hit the ball. It would make a pinging sound as it hit the ball, and it would send it off to the opposite side of the screen, where Maya would move her paddle and hit the ball back. Through the magic of electronics, the two of us were playing paddle tennis right there on the screen of the TV. I lunged for the ball, pushed the paddle too far, and missed. A big number one appeared on Maya's side of the screen.

"I got it!" she shouted.

And then the ball appeared again. I hunkered down now in front of the set and tried to settle into a more determined frame of mind. One to nothing, huh. We'll see about that.

Maya, it turned out, was quite good. She had played TV games before, although she hadn't played this particular model. And she raced her paddle back and forth across the screen, easily returning my shots. On the other hand, she was only six. It would seem that with a determined effort, considering my superior intellect, age, coordination and experience, that I ought to be able to beat the little rat. At this point it was already four to three.

The game, it turns out, goes just up to twenty-one. The first person to reach this number wins the game, and at that point, the game stops and the little ball no longer appears. You have to press a reset button to play again, and, when you do, the final score disappears, the ball comes back, and everything starts over.

Maya and I played about six games together. I quickly got the knack of it, and although she was quite good, I found that I could pretty consistently beat her, by scores of twenty-one to twelve, twenty-one to fifteen.

"Why don't you LET me win," Maya asked with great six-year-old logic.

"Okay," I said.

And so we did that for awhile. Pretty soon she had won just about as many as I had won before.

"I'm going upstairs to play with my dolls," she finally announced. And so she did, leaving me with just one paddle of a two paddle game, and a great addiction to continue.

I recruited Ann to play a few games with me, and I even tried my son Adam, who is four. But eventually, everyone got tired of playing and went to bed, leaving just me, the TV, and the Atari. I thought that surely I would now have to go to bed too.

But no.

It turned out that if you pressed a certain button on the side of the game, you could summon up a robot to play the left hand paddle. Recluses could play. People who wanted to play all night could play. For the robot was willing, and it could go on indefinitely, never complaining and never wanting to go to bed.

I pressed the button.

*   *   *

Let me tell you, this robot plays a mighty good game of paddle tennis. You hit it to the left and he scoots over and hits it back. You hit it to the right and he scoots the other way. You can try carom shots off the side walls if you wish, and the robot returns it with a smash right down the middle. You can try a smash yourself and the robot is there, returning it with a vicious topspin.

In fact, I found that the robot played a virtually perfect game of paddle tennis. There was only one shot that he was programmed to miss, and it was this very difficult shot that I found myself constantly trying to make. An across-the-board angle shot is what it was. You had to get the robot out of position, either on one side of the screen or the other, and then you had to hit the ball on the very corner of your paddle. If you got it, the ball would scoot sideways, and the computer was not fast enough to get across to chase it. He'd come close, barely miss, and the ball would bounce on by.

One point for me.

As we played, the robot and I, I found that I could only make this shot a very small percentage of the time. Usually, I'd hit the ball back straight, and then the game would continue until the opportunity came up again. Of course, waiting for just this opportunity, with the robot out of position on one side of the court, I'd get very nervous. And sometimes, the robot would simply put a very easy shot right past me.

I lost the first game to the robot by a score of twenty-one to nine. And I lost the second game twenty-one to eight. The third game, however, I steeled myself for a major effort and played with all the skill and cunning that I could muster. Briefly, I got ahead of the robot, but then panicked and made a few mistakes. I got ahead again, and for a while it appeared that I might actually win. It was fourteen to ten my favor, then fifteen.

And then I fell apart.

The robot ran off eight straight points in a row, ruthlessly, and suddenly I was down by nineteen to fifteen. It took only a few more minutes to polish me off at twenty-one - sixteen.

I was sweating now. Had the ability of the robot improved during the last five points of that game, or had it been my imagination? I had made cross shot after cross shot, but either the robot had not been fully out of position, or else it had been programmed to move faster as the game progressed.

I tried a fourth game and lost, twenty-one to five. I was totally disoriented.

But then I braced myself for one final game. I would catch the robot early, when it was slow and fat, and I would get such a lead that the robot could never catch up, no matter how good it got.

Sure enough, in the early part of this last game, I made one cross-court shot after the other. The robot —and I had a good vision of him now in my mind— trudged breathlessly across the court, unable to move his bulk with the necessary speed, and he would miss.

One point for me.

I reeled off point after point and pretty soon had it up to eight to nothing before I finally lost a point. Then I lost another, and I began to wonder. Was I getting shaken? Was I getting a little arm weary? I got a point and the robot got one. The robot got another one. It was nine to three.

And then, once again, I just fell apart. Damn this robot, I thought. Damn electronic things that just never get tired, that never get headaches or blurred vision. Damn them. It was ten to five, then eleven to eight. The robot was catching up.

I played desperately. I tried sneaky spin shots and double angle shots. But it was to no avail. The robot was bigger, stronger, and it would go on forever. I, on the other hand, was mortal. In the end, I would be reduced to nothing.

*   *   *

At three o'clock in the morning, in the darkest part of the night, I woke up. The sweats were gone. The shaking over my final defeat was gone. I heard Ann breathing heavily beside me and I heard the sounds of the crickets in the woods outside.

Without any hesitation, I got out of bed. I did not put on a robe. I did not put on any slippers. I simply padded downstairs, turned on the Atari game in the living room, and methodically beat the living daylights out of the robot.

The score was twenty-one to six.

Then I turned the thing back off and walked back upstairs.

Funny. I felt no emotions about my victory. But for the rest of the night I slept like a rock.

An Afternoon in
The Hammock

There is a hammock stretched between two trees in my yard, and sometimes I go and lie in it to retreat from the travails of the day.

Yesterday afternoon was such a time. It was three fifteen, and the sun was shining and the birds were chirping, and it seemed like a fine idea to just settle in the old hammock and maybe take a little rest before dinner. As an afterthought, I decided to bring the morning copy of the New York Times with me to the hammock. It had been some time since I had been able to find out what was going on in the world. What with the newspaper I publish, swimming, jogging, and going to dinner parties in this lovely resort, I had sort of gotten out of touch.

I lay down, and I opened the Times, and this is what I read.

On the front page I read that the Senate was acting to lift the arms ban on the Turks.

Also on the front page was a suggestion by a Missouri man that there had been a plot to murder Dr. Martin Luther King ten years ago; that Tito was warning the Cubans to watch themselves in Africa; and that Town Hall, the Manhattan concert hall, was going to close its doors because of too much competition.

On the front page of the second section was a picture of a new Arabesque Mosque that is going to be built on East 97th Street. It will be about thirty stories tall, to judge by the photograph.

"We think this will be a showplace for modern Islamic architecture and a major tourist attraction in the City," said Robert Thabit, the legal advisor to

141

the Islamic Center.

The twenty-million-dollar building, it turned out, is being paid for with money from Libya, Kuwait, Saudi Arabia and Iraq. Which had, in turn, been paid for by our money at the gas pump. It was thoughtful of them to return this money to us in such an unusual way. But it's better than nothing, I suppose.

Inside the paper, there was a story about a little baby girl who had just been born in England. This little baby had spent a good part of her pre-natal life in a test tube, where doctors had fiddled with the mother's egg and the father's sperm to get the thing started. After awhile, the doctors transferred the baby from the test tube into the mother's womb, where it then came to term and was born the usual way.

There was a discussion, in the Times, about other embryos that had been experimented with between conception and birth. There had been a good deal of this concerning cows, sheep, goats and rabbits.

"Experiments with freezing livestock embryos have been intended to facilitate shipment of new, highly productive strains."

Apparently, there were farmers around the world who wanted a certain strain of livestock, but couldn't afford to have it shipped. Instead, they'd freeze the embryo and ship that. It weighed a lot less. Then they'd thaw it out.

"The shipping of frozen embryos has largely supplanted an earlier practice, in which rabbits were used to transport cattle embryos," the Times wrote. "The chemistry of the rabbit uterus is sufficiently similar to that of a cow to sustain such an embryo for four or five days, long enough to fly samples of exotic strains as far as Australia."

Now this presented all sorts of ideas for humanity. Want to plan a family? Put some eggs and sperm together in a test tube, wait until you get an embryo, then freeze everything. Once a year, you can thaw a child out.

Another idea that comes to mind is planning on a trip to Europe. Can't afford the air fare? Why not go when your children are frozen? A family of six could go as two adults and a box. Why not?

I rolled over a bit in the hammock to ponder this new bit of information. And then I saw the article about bias against homosexuals.

The Mayor of Hartford had gotten in his car and driven off for Kennedy Airport and a flight to Greece for a vacation. Then, after he left, the City Council in Hartford had gotten together and had quietly passed this law banning bias against homosexuals. The Mayor, it turned out, had been opposed to this law and had said so. But the City Council knew that if the Mayor was out of the country for five days, then they could pass it without his vetoing it. And so they voted it secretly while he was gone.

The Mayor's plane, however, was delayed for seven hours. And during that time the Mayor heard about the City Council's vote, had the document brought to the airport in a car, and thereupon vetoed it anyway.

"Apparently, they passed it last night because they thought I would be heading for Greece," he said, adding, "but the Lord works in mysterious ways."

Not far from this article was a story about two policemen who were thrown in jail because they would not reveal a confidential source. And on another page there was a story about a newspaperman in New Jersey who violated a confidence.

There was another interesting story on page six. In the town of Burnley, England, a 42-year-old man named Frank Clifford had formed an organization called the Burnley Dog Owners' Action Committee in order to protest a Town Council law prohibiting dogs in the parks.

The Town Council law did not prohibit dogs in all the parks, but in just 141 acres of parkland where children tended to play soccer and other games. They felt that the dogs would "foul the footpáths," and that this would be an unhealthful situation.

Mr. Clifford on behalf of all the dog owners of the Town has felt otherwise, and on their behalf he has deliberately violated the law by taking his dogs, Honey and Mandy, into the off-limits part of the park. He has been arrested, and now he is preparing to go to jail rather than obey the law.

All across Britain, people have taken up the cause of Mr. Clifford and his dogs. There is a public outcry in the press as Mr. Clifford prepares for Brixton Prison.

"(In England)" the Times wrote, paraphrasing writer Douglas Sutherland, "a gentleman looks on his wife with kindly patronage and his children with qualified affection. (But a gentleman's) deepest affection is. . .reserved for his dogs."

Meanwhile, on page two, there was a story that Christina Onassis was going to marry a 40-year-old unemployed Russian shipping official. Ms. Onassis had denied it, but it seemed pretty certain. She and Sergei Kauzov were going to get married on Tuesday and settle in a two-room apartment in Moscow. Christina was going to shop and cook and wash the dishes. Christina is worth $500 million.

"If they are allowed to live abroad, there will be no problem," a family friend said. "But if she has to live in Moscow all the time, it will be sad."

On another page, I learned that a woman who wanted a test tube baby was suing her doctor and the hospital for 1.5 million dollars. The doctor apparently had poured the test tube baby out.

144

There was also the story about a man who was being sued for refusing to have an operation. This man, David Shimp, has been asked to donate 21 ounces of bone marrow to a sick cousin, Robert McFall. McFall needed the bone marrow in order to live, and his cousin, David Shimp, was the only person who could give it to him. He had to be related.

"Judge John P. Flaherty, Jr. of Allegheny County Common Pleas Court," the Times said, "directed defense attorneys for David Shimp to file a brief setting forth the reasons why Mr. Shimp should not be ordered to give about 21 ounces of bone marrow to Robert McFall."

The brief was to be presented tomorrow.

Out at San Clemente Island in California, Navy officials, reporters and newsmen looked on as an American submarine test fired the first two Tomahawk cruise missiles. Nothing happened.

"Failure in the past increases the probability of success in the future," said Secretary of Defense Harold Brown.

This whole business was making me sleepy, I thought. What was going on in the world?

And then I saw the article about the man in San Francisco who was suing a girl for standing him up.

According to the news item, Tom Horsley had made a dinner date with Alyn Chesselet in San Jose, where she lived. Tom left his office, drove fifty miles, and she WASN'T THERE. He was suing her for seventeen cents a mile for his 100-mile round-trip, and for two hours of waiting time at $8.50 an hour, which was what he usually charged as an accountant. He also was suing her for court costs.

Mr. Horsley said in court that he had made the date two weeks before and that she did not call him to tell him she wouldn't be there. He also said that she could certainly surmise that he would be leaving work early on the day of the date in order to make the drive, and that she knew that his telephone answering service did not accept collect calls.

"She certainly did not make a good faith effort," Tom Horsely told the judge.

"I hope somebody has some legal basis for this," Judge Richard Figone said, before reserving judgment for a later date.

And so, I fell asleep.

Lord of the Flies

About eleven o'clock in the morning the other day, I was sitting in the front office of DAN'S PAPERS, staring out into the street, not doing much. The office was busy at that hour, with telephone ringing and people bustling this way and that, but it was quiet for me, and I was just enjoying the view.

A yellow Buick pulled up out by the picket fence, and three people got out and headed up the lawn toward the office. They were a well-dressed man and woman, each about thirty, and a little boy, perhaps four years old. As they came up onto the front porch, I could see the boy's eyes darting this way and that, sizing up the building, the shrubbery, the whole lay of the land. His mind was racing on ahead.

The man held the front door open for the woman and she walked in to our small outer lobby. But the boy refused to follow. He stood on the porch there and crossed his arms.

"Come on," the father said.

"I'm not going. I don't wanna."

The man looked longingly at the woman, who had stopped there in the outer lobby.

"He doesn't want to come in," the man said.

"May I help you?" the receptionist asked.

"We want to place a classified ad," the woman replied. "Just a minute."

She turned and walked back out on the front porch.

"Why don't you want to go in?" she asked the boy.

"I just don't wanna."

"Would you wait out here, and I'll just go in?"

"No."

"Daddy will wait with you on the front porch."

"No."

"How about some ice cream?" the man asked. "What if I promise to get you some ice cream after we go in here?" He turned to the woman. "There's got to be an ice cream parlor near by."

The woman came back into the front lobby, but no further. "Is there an ice cream parlor near by?" she asked the receptionist.

"Right down the street, the Candy Kitchen."

The woman went back outside and relayed this information to her husband.

"I'll get you a chocolate ice cream sundae after we go inside," the man said to the boy.

"I want an ice cream SODA," the boy said.

"A soda then. Anything."

"And I want it NOW. BEFORE we go inside."

The man looked at the woman, and the two of them shrugged.

"Okay," the man said. "We'll get you a chocolate ice cream soda, and then we'll go inside."

And the three of them turned around and walked back across the front lawn to their car.

They did come back, about forty-five minutes later. The boy looked just as troubled and as grim as he did before, and once again he halted just before the front door.

"You said you would go in after you had an ice cream soda," the man said.

"I changed my mind," the boy announced.

Again, the woman came back outside, and again they tried to persuade the little boy to wait on the front porch or out in the car with the father. Then, after about five minutes of getting nowhere with this line of talk, they gave up the attempt, went back out to their car and drove off.

I never did find out what kind of classified ad they wanted to place.

Georgica Pond Causeway

The State of New York unveiled plans yesterday for a broad eight-lane causeway across Georgica Pond. About two hundred stunned residents of East Hampton attended the unveiling of the plan, which took place in the State office building on Main Street, Riverhead. It is expected there will be public hearings on this plan before it can go much farther. Surprisingly, most of the State officials seemed optimistic about its chances. The local people, however, seemed dead set against it.

"We think there is a need for a causeway across Georgica Pond," said Brian Dangerfield, Assistant Director of Public Information for the State Department of Transportation.

"As you can see," Dangerfield continued, "the causeway is designed to solve a very specific traffic problem. The problem of driving on the Montauk Highway in the summertime where it passes Georgica Pond.

"The Montauk Highway on summer weekends is disastrously overloaded. People who know better simply don't take the Highway. They take the back roads on the weekend. But at Georgica Pond they have absolutely no choice. There simply are no back roads to get around the Pond, and for nearly two miles, there is NO WAY to avoid driving on the Highway. The solution, of course, is to build this causeway, linking the back roads on either side of the pond."

A number of people, in the back row of the assembly, applauded Mr. Dangerfield at this point. But observers noticed that those people applauding were all former construction contractors, the men who were last employed building the Westhampton Beach jetties.

"This is the most cockamamie idea I've ever heard of," a resident of Amagansett said.

"No, it is not," Dangerfield continued. "It is a very real idea, and it has been very really worked on by the Engineers up in Albany. They have no doubt it can be done. And done well, too, I might add. Incidentally, the funds for the Causeway are already available. They were approved years ago for the Sunrise Superhighway Extension which, as you know, was finally killed by Governor Carey. The money is just floating around. All we have to do is use it."

Mr. Dangerfield then proceeded to explain the details of the construction of the causeway. It was to be eight lanes wide with a center island, all made of concrete. It would float on fiberglass pontoons anchored in the muck at the bottom of the Pond "for the ecology, so the fish can swim unencumbered," and it would be toll free, for the moment anyway. Toll booths were to be built on both sides of the pond in the event that someday, for a local charity or something, it was decided to charge a toll for crossing the Pond.

"There won't be any fishing allowed off the Causeway," Mr. Dangerfield said. "And we won't have a pedestrian walk either. We don't want any lawsuits. This is strictly for the automobile."

Mr. Dangerfield then went on to say that a special referendum was going to be set up to see if local

150

residents wanted the causeway or not. Actually, the referendum was not going to see WHETHER they wanted it, but WHERE they wanted it. There would be just two choices and the referendum question would read "which do you prefer, choice A or choice B."

Dangerfield explained the different choices.

"In choice A, the Causeway will cross the pond east to west just about in the middle. It will hook up at Main Street, Wainscott on the western shore, cut through the prestigious Georgica Association, and then cross the pond to hook up with Briar Patch Road leading into Georgica Road. This is, indeed, the cheaper of the two choices, but it does involve tearing down about a half dozen forty-room mansions along the pond there to make room for the cloverleafs.

"Choice B is further south. It is more costly, but it is also more picturesque, running along right over the beach. The Causeway begins on the west bank at Beach Lane, Wainscott, runs parallel to the ocean for about a mile, and then hooks up with West End Road on the eastern bank. It would involve condemning about a dozen big mansions, including those of Juan Trippe and the late Peter Revson. It does, however, afford the possibility of building a boardwalk along the beach there at a later date, perhaps with some penny arcades and ferris wheels."

The contingent from East Hampton sat through this hearing in a sort of depressed silence for the most part. One observer even stooped to calling it a stupor. Few of the residents spoke. But afterwards, in interviews with reporters, it was apparent that most of the residents were simply overwhelmed into speechlessness with the audacity of the idea.

"A Georgica Pond bypass?" one older resident kept repeating over and over again.

"Somebody has got to get a punch in the nose," a younger man said. He stood around angrily with his fists clenched, but he did nothing about it.

Perhaps most interested in the plan was Peter Pippin of East Hampton, who is also head of the Stop the Highways Citizens Association. But Mr. Pippin was reticent.

"No comment," Mr. Pippin said. "I have no comment until I have presented this proposal to the board." Mr. Pippin did seem to be containing himself, however.

At the end of the meeting, Mr. Dangerfield spoke briefly about some of the other plans the Department of Transportation has in the works. He spoke about the negotiations in progress with the Walt Disney people who were interested in purchasing the Suffolk County Air Force Base in Westhampton for some reason or other. And he also talked briefly about the planned Mecox Bay Hydrofoil.

"The hydrofoil is only in the drawing board stage," Mr. Dangerfield said. "After all, it is possible to take the Head of Pond Road bypass to get around Mecox. No problem there with the Montauk Highway."

Story From The Beach

It was a beautiful beach day. Down the way, sitting on a blanket, was a pretty blonde woman with two children. The little girl was about six, the boy about three. The boy played happily in the sand, sometimes digging a hole, sometimes cuddling a large, stuffed bunny pillow that had been brought for the occasion.

After awhile, a large Labrador retriever appeared from over the dune. The children expressed delight at seeing such a beautiful sleek dog, and the Lab obliged the children by walking happily over and wagging his tail. He allowed himself to be patted.

But then the dog saw the bunny pillow. With one swift motion, he picked it up and trotted off with it in his mouth. About thirty feet away, he stopped and looked to see the confusion he had created. The grown woman was on her feet, the girl was shouting, and the little boy was crying, "the dog took my bunny rabbit — the dog took my bunny rabbit."

The dog simply wagged his tail. He thought it was a great game. He held the bunny rabbit gently in his mouth.

The blonde woman put the older girl in charge of the younger boy and proceeded to walk slowly after the Lab.

"Here, boy," she said. "Here, boy."

But the dog did not respond. He trotted off another ten feet and stopped.

"Come on, boy," she said. "Come on. Over here. Come over here."

This continued on for quite some time.

The woman tried all sorts of things to get the dog to come back. She tried calling a variety of names, such as Rover, King, Fred, Duke, Duchess, etc., but the dog would have none of it.

She tried running straight at the dog, but the dog would gracefully sidestep her and trot away.

She tried throwing small rocks at the dog. But she missed.

She even tried sitting down, with the hopes that the dog would come to her. But his didn't work either.

I was just about to get up to help when the woman hit upon the one thing that got her what she wanted.

She pointed an index finger at the dog.

"Bad," she said. "Bad dog."

A mournful expression came over the dog's face.

"Bad dog. Shame. Shame on you for being such a bad dog. Bad."

Still pointing, she walked forcefully over to the dog with long steps. The dog dropped the bunny rabbit just as she arrived. He was totally repentant.

The woman examined the bunny rabbit, and found it unharmed.

"Good dog," she said. "That's a good dog." She patted him.

And they lived happily ever after. At least for the rest of the afternooon.

Mother Nature as Seen by Walt Disney

Up in an apple tree, a large cat sits unsteadily on a branch and waits attentively. Watching from a picnic table, the people wait as well. He is a domestic cat, belonging to the neighbor across the way, and he has a black diamond marking on his forehead and a small red ribbon around his neck. He is not quite full grown.

A bird lands. A sparrow. It alights on one of the very outer twigs of the apple tree and hops lightly from one branch to another, unaware. The cat's ears draw forward and his tail swishes excitedly back and forth. He concentrates, goes into a crouch.

"Look out," someone at the picnic table whispers. But it is only a whisper.

The cat springs, and immediately he's in trouble. The bird is gone, flown away just a split instant after the start of the spring, and the cat has now got himself into trouble, or more exactly, thin branches. The tree gives way beneath his feet, and he staggers and falls, grabbing desperately at the lower branches, scrabbling for a hold. Finally, he gets it. Upside down, hanging on different skinny branches with different feet, he sways delicately, under control now, and trying to figure out what to do next. Slowly, gently, and with great care, the cat finds one strong branch after another and makes his way back toward the center of the tree, where the branches are strong and the going considerably easier. There are no birds in the middle of the tree. They all land on the delicate corners of the tree. But the cat settles down anyway, content for the moment, and waits for the next round with the sparrows.

"Wasn't that funny?" someone says at the picnic table.

"Shhh. Don't make too much noise. You'll scare him away."

"I think another bird is going to land."

Everyone sits back and continues eating hamburgers and drinking cokes, slowly and in slow motion, so they won't disturb this scene that is right out of a Walt Disney movie, unfolding in front of them.

Indeed, all that is missing is the music. That, and the happy narrator. You can just see it. The cat sits and waits, and the music goes nervous and worrisome, then the cat springs, there is a crashing of cymbals, and then some very funny, off-key chord.

"Whoops!" the narrator laughs. "And Harry has missed again. But does he give up? No, he doesn't. He'll just get his footing a little bit better, whoops! And now he'll go back and try it again, HA, HA!"

What they don't tell you is that when they made the movie, they left out all the film clips where the cat actually GOT the bird. That, after all, is what this whole thing was really about. Eating live birds.

Walt Disney made his famous nature movies during the early 1950's. There was Herman the Lion, who couldn't seem to catch any deer. And there was Peter the Porcupine, who scared off the mean, old snake so the snake didn't catch anything either. From what you could see of these Walt Disney movies, it was a wonder everybody looked so healthy and well-fed, because, if you believe what you saw, nobody ever actually ate anybody. Although heaven knows they tried.

It was also during this post-war period that packaged meats and frozen foods came into their own. You no longer saw a chicken hanging upside down in the butcher shop. You saw it, instead, sitting in the cold case wrapped in clear cellophane (later, plastic), looking very much like it would look when it came out of the oven.

Shortly after all of this, everyone got very interested in saving the wildlife, and this is one of the big issues going today.

I wonder if there is any connection with all of this.

The fact is, being a bird, or a lion, or a giraffe, or a sheep out there in the wilds of nature means very much taking the risk of winding up as someone's dinner. How would you like it? You wake up in the morning, and you say, well, I'm hungry again, so I guess I'll have to go out there and find somebody to eat. And so you go out of your cave, or your hole, or your nest, or whatever it is, and you start looking around for something a little smaller than yourself and perhaps a little slower that you can pounce upon and eat. The littler creatures do, indeed, exist. In fact, you just ate one yesterday. But then again, so do the bigger creatures exist. You just got away from one yesterday. You go out and you think about all this. What are your chances? Oh, about 50 percent that you'll get eaten. You're nothing special, after all is said and done. And so you go out looking, because you are, after all, very hungry. And that very afternoon, while you're sitting very quietly behind a tree, you see him: a creature about ten times the size of you, that you know is faster than you, that has yellow eyes, fangs and happens to be looking right at you.

"Such is life," is perhaps what you say as you turn tail and run, filled with fear and hope that you may live to see another day.

"And this time, Herman the Lion actually GETS him," the narrator says, voice over.

You get eaten alive.

If the Supreme Court of the United States were to review the case of Mother Nature and her various laws, they would probably condemn the whole thing to a fate worse than death. For millions of years now, no, for even longer than that, living creatures have been going out and killing, IN COLD BLOOD, if you will, other creatures without any rhyme or reason other than the pure gut lust of hunger. It's been disgraceful. And worse still, Walt Disney and his gang have been trying to gloss over the whole thing as if it were some kind of fable.

Yesterday, I went walking through the wildlife zoo they have over in Manorville, New York. There were sheep living there, and lambs and goats and horses and camels and monkeys and flamingoes and seals. They were all behind fences, of one kind or another. Although some were simply in large pens where there was plenty of room to run around.

"Isn't it a shame they keep all those wild animals cooped up like this," I overheard someone say.

"A shame?" I said. "These animals are PROTECTED. They don't have to WORRY. Here they are, they don't have to chase around trying to eat anybody. They don't have the problem of somebody latching onto one of their hind legs and eating them. They're fed from a box. If they're sick, they get medicine. A SHAME, Madam. You've got it all wrong."

The woman looked at me funny, and she walked away. The animals looked at me, and they just

158

looked dumb. They didn't appreciate any of it.

I thought about the game preserves, the large thousand-acre tracts where animals were still in the wild, still getting up in the morning and going out to eat each other, still living in fear and terror, and I began to wonder...how quickly would it be possible to pave all this over?

Dr. Joyce Brothers
And
The Weather

At six o'clock Friday evening, I decided to call the weather bureau. It was sunny and clear at that time, and there had been a beautiful sunset, but I really needed to know what the weather would be like for the weekend. I was especially interested in Sunday afternoon, because at that time, I was planning a giant outdoor Halloween costume party for adults and kids, and I needed to know it wouldn't rain all over the costumes. Actual Halloween trick or treating would not take place for two days after that.

I dialed WE 9-1212, and this is what I was told. I learned the current Deer Park temperature was forty-eight, the barometer was thirty point o nine and rising, the humidity was twenty percent, the wind was at five miles an hour, and there was a zero possibility of rain through tomorrow night, which would be Saturday. Then, the weatherman said, "Dial Dr. Joyce Brothers at 936-4444, and hear her discuss a subject that is of interest and importance to your life. That number again is 936-4444.

In other words, the weatherman was not saying anything about whether or not it would rain on Sunday.

But then there was this business about Dr. Joyce Brothers. Well, the most important subject of my life at that moment was whether it would rain or not on my Halloween party. What the hell. It was only a message unit. Certainly it was worthwhile to hear what Dr. Joyce Brothers had to say. I dialed the number.

"This is Dr. Joyce Brothers. Today's topic? How to relieve stress on the job."

But what about Sunday?

"Stress, if left unchecked, can lead to backache, tension, headache, muscle aches and ulcers. Stress and its side effects cost American industry anywhere from ten to fifteen million dollars a year. Too often, bosses will transfer their pressures to people who work with them, and they, in turn, pass it along to others."

This had nothing to do with my Halloween party.

"You can stop this vicious cycle by employing some easily learnable techniques. Instant relaxation is one. It consists of closing your eyes, taking a deep breath, exhaling and saying the word RELAX."

This cost me a message unit? This cost me a message unit?

"Just this exercise alone, when repeated for a few minutes a day can help. Also, there is a deep muscle relaxation drill where you take off your shoes, loosen your tie or belt and stretch down on a chair, sofa or floor for twenty or thirty minutes."

But what about Halloween? Would Dr. Brothers refer me to ANOTHER expert at the end of her recording? Maybe Henny Youngman?

"These are only emergency techniques. Nevertheless, its a beginning, and a step in the right direction."

Joyce Brothers hung up.

As a matter of fact, I WAS getting a headache, a little muscle tension and maybe an ulcer. And so, I took off my shoes, loosened my shirt and lay down on the floor. I knew right away it would not rain on Sunday.

The
Jaws Letter

The Office of the Chief of Police
June 20, 1975

To the Editor of Dan's Papers:

With the movie JAWS now playing at the East Hampton Cinema, I would think it would be a good idea, at this time, to allay the fears of some of your readers that a big, man-eating shark might eat them up during the summer.

As you know, the movie is about just such a man-eating shark, and it describes how half a dozen people lost their lives as they swam around in the ocean just off our shores. The movie further describes how we government officials are unable to cope with this shark, and it alleges that we cover up every incident in which a tourist is eaten up by a fish.

All of these allegations are false in every respect. For one thing, the number of people eaten by the man-eating shark is nowhere near a half dozen a day as shown in the movie. Through careful feeding of the man-eater, we have now reduced the number of people lost to the shark in any given day to just one, or at the most, two. And for this, I might add, we owe a vote of thanks to every member of this police force, including both the present membership and those deceased members of the force, may they rest in peace, who gave their lives so that others may swim. Our force, during the last month or two, has worked night and day continuously feeding the shark raw meat so that he is constantly well-fed, and not in a serious mood to eat swimmers. This feeding, conducted by helicopter, has been made possible by the generosity of virtually all of our local butchers, who have sacrificed thousands and thousands of pounds of raw meat they might otherwise have sold at a profit to the general public. It is this sort of unselfish generosity, which makes America the great nation that it is today.

With the arrival of the summer tourists, we are hopeful that the amount of meat donated for the feeding of the shark might double or even triple, so that even less than one tourist a day might be eaten by the man-eating shark.

To this end, I would ask your readers to please join in this raw meat drive, just as your readership responded so generously during World War II with contributions of tin, rubber and bacon fat. Anyone with leftover meat at the dinner table, or with uncooked meat (preferably), is asked to pack it up and bring it down to the police station in

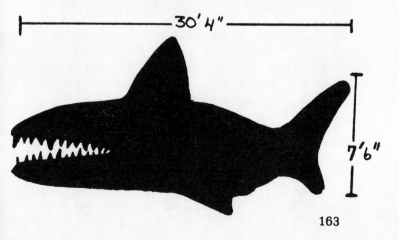

30' 4"

7'6"

Bridgehampton between the hours of nine and five for collection. The man-eating shark has shown a distinct preference for lamb chops and spare ribs, if that should make any difference.

One final note. Due to the great help of marine biologist Alfred Silverton, we have been able to train the man-eating shark to eat his meals in different places at different times. On Mondays, Wednesdays and Fridays, he is fed in the ocean, off Main Beach, in the center of town. But on Tuesdays, Thursdays and Saturdays, the shark has been trained to take his meals over in the shallow waters of Peconic Bay. On these days of Tuesdays, Thursdays and Saturdays, it is absolutely safe to swim in the ocean, since we can positively assure you the shark is in the bay. On Sundays, incidentally, the shark naps.

We would like your readership to take note of the silhouette of the shark reproduced on page 163.

There are many large sharks swimming around in the ocean, and although other sharks might come up and gnaw playfully on your arm or something, this particular shark is the only one which will actually eat you all up.

As time goes by, Dr. Silverton assures me he is more and more able to teach the man-eating shark tricks, thus heading him down the path toward domestication. Already, Dr. Silverton reports, the man-eater will come when he is called, sit, stay, and clap his fins playfully after each meal.

Tourists in the Hamptons should be assured that with the increased meat drive, we can cause the shark to give up eating swimmers altogether. And, in the event the meat drive does not live up to standards, and there simply is not enough meat available, your readership should know this police department, every one of us, has taken a vow of personal sacrifice.

We here at the police department are determined to make every tourist's summer vacation a happy and enjoyable one, no matter who has to get eaten in the process.

Sincerely,
Martin Brody
Chief of Police, Bridgehampton

Yom Kipper

Sunday evening, October 3, was the eve of the Jewish holiday of Yom Kippur. In Riverhead and Sag Harbor, as throughout much of Long Island, cars were parked on the streets in front of the local synagogues. It was a stormy night. And flood conditions prevailed throughout much of the Island.

In East Hampton, however, the cars lining the streets were not at the local Jewish Center on Woods Lane. They were, instead, on Main Street in front of the First Presbyterian Church.

The First Presbyterian Church?

Inside that magnificent church, which is perhaps the oldest and most beautiful church in the Hamptons, there was to be heard responsive reading in Hebrew. A passerby, puzzled by the unusual music coming from the church, could have looked through the window that rainy night and seen a rabbi and a cantor leading a congregation of four hundred through the traditional prayer of Kol Nidre.

The Presbyterian minister of the church, Reverend Fredrick W. Schulz, could be seen sitting in the balcony of his church, looking down on this large flock of worshippers who belonged, under normal circumstances, at the Jewish Center of the Hamptons around the corner.

But these were not ordinary circumstances.

Contarary to tradition, which said that on Yom Kippur the weather was always sunny and bright, it was raining as hard as Noah's Flood. Cars were stalled in puddles along the side of the roads, and little metal oil lamps marked the worst of them. Route 114, between East Hampton and Sag Harbor, became impassable where it dips down to that low point beneath the railroad bridge. The water was three feet deep, and the police had to set up detours. By five o'clock in the afternoon, it became apparent to Evan Frankel, President of the Jewish Center, that services could not be held on Woods Lane. Flood conditions prevailed on the property of the Jewish Center, and the giant striped tent which had been set up in the back yard to accommodate the crowds of Jews that come to the Yom Kippur service every year simply covered a small flood of water.

What to do? After a brief discussion, it was decided to call Reverend Schulz of the nearby Presbyterian Church to see if he could help out. Rabbi Friedlander was called upon to do the job.

"Worship in our church," Reverend Schulz had said. "You will be warm and dry. A house of worship is a house of worship."

And so it was. At seven o'clock, members of the Jewish Congregation dressed in their Sunday finest, arrived through the rain and darkness to the Jewish Center on Woods Lane, only to find people standing out in the rain with umbrellas and flashlights.

"Turn around. We are worshipping at the Presbyterian Church on Main Street. We're flooded out here."

*   *   *

On the pulpit, the Torah, the Jewish book of laws, lay open beneath the giant Presbyterian cross on the front wall. Some worshippers found Jewish prayer books. Others found Christian prayer books. And so they proceeded through a marvelous evening of rain and brotherly love in East Hampton.

Fireworks Bash

At five minutes to ten in the evening, the first of George Plimpton's Bastille Day fireworks blasted off of the Atlantic Ocean beach with a great thump and headed toward the night sky.

A great cheer rose up from the five hundred or so people sitting around on blankets on the broad front lawn of Freddy and George Plimpton's Wainscott house a hundred yards to the north. For the fireworks, held every year as a tradition at the Plimpton home, had been delayed for some reason for nearly an hour. And the guests on the lawn—perhaps a majority of the glitterai in the Hamptons that weekend, and including Kurt Vonnegut, Norman Mailer, Betty Friedan, columnist Joseph Kraft, Mike Burke, writers Gail Greene, Nora Ephron and Jim Bouton—had become impatient with waiting.

"George," someone shouted over the microphone at nine thirty, "if you don't start the fireworks soon, all the people will go home."

George Plimpton was down on the dunes with the Jim Grucci Fireworks Company of Bellport, and the California Pyrotechnics Company from California, and just perhaps they got the message. Perhaps they hurried a little too much. Certainly, they misjudged the wind.

"The whole thing was poorly planned," East Hampton Town Fire Inspector David DiSunno was to say the next day after the injuries. "There were people down on the beach who shouldn't have been there."

The first of the fireworks burst high in the sky, a great orange display. And then there was the sound of the report, and the glow of the trailing comet.

"They seem awful close," someone sitting on a blanket said.

A second firework went up through the mortar and into the sky. A third followed and then a fourth. These early fireworks were most unusual and were, in fact, original fireworks created especially for the Plimpton show, and for a later International Show in Monte Carlo. Mr. DiSunno was to call these early fireworks "experimental." George Plimpton was later to deny they were anything of the sort.

The second batch of fireworks exploded in the sky above us, but one which seemed delayed floated toward the earth. Everyone instinctively pulled back, and the firework went off not fifty feet above the assembled crowd. It made a tremendous bang.

I remember moving instinctively when this firework came so close, and I could hear people murmuring all around me. I was seated on a blanket with other people on the southeast corner of the lawn farthest from the house. Earlier, there had been the picnic, the Peggy Herra Dance Group, the mimes, unicycle riders and jugglers, and now the fireworks. What was George doing?

More fireworks went off, and people began screaming. Bits of ash and junk were landing amid the crowd, and the crowd began moving around. And then a bright ball of fire, the comet part of one of these "experimental" fireworks came down ten feet from me in the middle of the crowd.

My God, it will explode, were my first thoughts. I grabbed my bottle of wine and the blanket and stood up, pressing back toward the house. The glowing comet, about half a foot across, throbbed in the lawn. Something was horribly wrong.

"Stop the fireworks!" someone shouted over the loudspeaker. "My God, they're landing on the people! Stop the fireworks, George."

"Get up to the house," I yelled to everyone on my

169

blanket.

Some people were rooted to the spot, staring wide-eyed at the comet. Others ran, as I and my friends did, toward the bar and the safety of the house.

But was it safe? A few more fireworks went off before George stopped the shooting, and some of these flew over the house and landed on the lawn behind. Mike Roselle, the Bridgehampton Fire Chief who was also on the scene, later said he had gotten a black casing that had landed on the house.

"It's a wooden house," he said. "They were all very lucky." The black casing, he said, he would keep in the back seat of his car, if anybody wanted to see it.

The shooting had stopped. The beam of a white searchlight waved back and forth from the dunes across the way. George had heard.

"Would Dr. David Pearce, David Pearce, please report to the microphone area," someone shouted over the P.A. "It's an emergency."

George bounded through the brush and ran through the crowd toward the microphone. Apparently, someone had been burned on the arm and someone else in the eye. But nothing was serious. They would be all right.

"The fireworks committee apologizes to you all," Plimpton said. "But this is only a delay. We've misjudged the wind, and the wind is carrying the fireworks over the house. We will simply reset the mortars, point them out over the ocean, and will continue in about ten minutes."

And then George was gone, back through the crowd across the field and over the dune. There were people on the beach between the dunes and the ocean. Unauthorized people who had gotten past the police guards. So Plimpton and Grucci could not adjust the mortars too much or they would put these people on the beach in danger. They would, instead, adjust the mortars just a bit.

Back at the lawn, some of the guests chose to take this moment to leave the scene. But others, including this reporter, decided to put their blankets down and return to their seats. At this point, Chief Mike Roselle, from his engine on the dunes, radioed the firehouse for two pumpers. One of these he would station alongside the Plimpton house to protect the people and the property in case of fire.

The two people who were burned were taken by private car to the Southampton Hospital. The rest of the people for the most part settled back down.

And then the first of the pumpers arrived. At the entrance to the house, people employed by the Plimptons tried to keep the fire truck off the lawn. They failed. The fire truck would be stationed where the fire chief thought it best.

BOOM.

The fireworks had started again. And this time they seemed more over the dunes, more in the place where they ought to be. Still, however, they drifted overhead toward the house before they burned out. Pink ones and green ones, sizzlers and bangers, raining down shreds of cardboard, plastic and paper on the guests below.

Something hot landed on the back of my right hand. I shook it, and whatever it was flew off. But I could see nothing.

"Anyone got a flashlight?" I asked the people I was with. Nobody did. I went back to watching the rest of the display, and tried to forget about my fear of the earlier bombardment.

Out on the dunes, sparks from a spent firework rained down and sizzled in the sand among the mortars of Grucci's "grand finale." Grucci sent a man in to remove the sparks by hand, but Fire Inspector David DiSunno had seen enough.

"Hose it down," he yelled.

Water poured onto the grand finale. Whatever it was, it would never go off now.

"That's it," DiSunno said. "That's enough. Show's over. Hose it ALL down."

And that, dear readers, is how the 1979 Plimpton Bastille Day fireworks came to an end. Perhaps as much as a quarter of the whole display had been shot off. For the rest, however, it was hosed down by a jittery fire department, putting a stop to everything.

There was a sense of relief and anti-climax on the lawn at this point. Nothing further took place, actually, except a lot of nervous laughter, picking up of blankets and picnic baskets, confusion and movement toward the cars which had been so carefully parked by a hired police force on the back lawn. It was 10:30 p.m.

George Plimpton appeared, to say good night to some of his guests. He was sweating and seemed as shaken about the preceding events as everyone else.

"We could make an "I SURVIVED THE PLIMPTON FIREWORKS' T-shirt," I said, trying to lighten the evening. He laughed a little.

*   *   *

In the light of day, the next day, I spoke to George Plimpton about what had taken place. He had held his fireworks as a private party for a good number of years now, and had always asked me to respect that and not write about it which I did. But now, we had the demonstration shut down by the fire department, and two people injured and taken to the hospital.

"The people who were burned are all right, and that's the important thing." George said. "One is a friend of Cy Coleman's, and the other had a cinder in the eye. I've apologized to both of them. As for that one comet that came down, it was really one in a hundred thousand. The lifting charge was apparently not sufficient, and one of the salts

172

exploded at an odd angle. But at least it wasn't a maroon. That would have been very bad. There could have been an explosion."

I asked George about a report that the Grucci people had simply rushed things, arriving at seven in the evening when they usually arrive in the afternoon to set things up, and he did not think that this had been a factor.

"They were ready on time," he said. "We all simply misjudged the wind. It must have been twenty times as strong high up as it was on the ground. That was really the problem."

George seemed genuinely upset that his fireworks display had gotten so far out of hand.

"These fireworks were just supposed to be a service to friends and the local community. But when the invitation to attend it appears in the New York Post on Page Six, and people come from 100 miles away, what can you do? For instance, there was a rock band from Commack that appeared and wanted to play. They were perfectly nice, but you know they weren't invited.

"It really is a shame. The display is really loved mostly by the children. I think there were over 200 children there, what with the mimes and the unicycle and all. Oh well."

Would the fire departments issue Plimpton permission to hold fireworks again next year?

"Unless the area is roped off," Chief Mike Roselle of Bridgehampton said, "and unless the people who are in the area are authorized to do so, there won't be anybody."

Chief DiSunno, who also must sign permission, commented as well.

"I would not issue a license without them coming in and going over operating procedures beforehand."

"I doubt if I would do this again next year,"

Plimpton said. "I don't like coming back from the fireworks and seeing 1,000 people I'd never seen before. It's no longer a private event."

It was, however, a night to remember.

July
Crab Fishing

On the Fourth of July, I was lying on the beach in Bridgehampton with my daughter who is six. We were lying there, listening to the surf, to the children playing, to the occasional drone of an airplane flying by, and we were just dozing off to sleep. In this semi-conscious state, my daughter and I engaged in the following conversation. I felt it was worth recording.

"Daddy? When a crab bites you, does it hurt?"

"Crabs don't bite."

"I mean AFTER they bite."

"AFTER they bite?"

"AFTER they bite."

"When they bite you on the leg, when you make it better."

"Huh?"

"You put something on it. You know, that stuff? Does it hurt?"

"No, it doesn't hurt."

"Why do crabs bite?"

"Crabs don't bite. Go to sleep."

"Yes, they do. You just said you put that stuff on it, and it doesn't hurt."

"Well, it doesn't."

"Do you put a bandaid on it?"

"Yes. You put the stuff on it, and then you put a bandaid on it. It doesn't hurt."

Yes, it does."

"Look, crabs don't bite."

"Did a crab ever bite you?"

"No."

"Are there any crabs around here. On this beach?"

"Well, yes, I suppose so. You see them around. But they don't bite."

"Yes, they do."

"Look, they're more afraid of you than you are of them."

"Daddy?"

"What?"

"You know how I know crabs bite?"

"How?"

"Because, if they didn't bite you, there wouldn't be crabs."

"That doesn't make any sense. FISH don't bite, and yet there are fish."

"Yeah, but fist aren't SUPPOSED to bite you. You EAT fish."

Folk Singer on The Campaign Trail

On a cold day in late October, an old mail truck painted red, white and blue, stops on a downtown street in Syracuse. Three men get out, quickly fold down a portable stage and lights, then put up a music stand and chair. A small crowd gathers.

Then, while one of the men — Chris Johnson of East Hampton — tunes up his guitar, the others put leaflets, campaign stickers and buttons out on the end of the stage. The crowd starts to take them.

"Is Mr. Duryea going to be here?" someone in the crowd asks.

"Not today. But if you wait around, we'll have some songs and entertainment," says one of the men.

Chris Johnson looks up from his guitar. He has finished his tuning. "Who here is for Duryea?" he asks.

The crowd roars, and Chris Johnson, secure that he is among friends, begins to sing a song of his own composition.

When Perry started workin'
He was standin' in his boat,
His hand was at the wheel
And his smile just made you feel
He was everything that he was meant to be.
Chasin' round his lobsters
Like his father did before him,
Was somethin' that he just came by...
naturally.

CHORUS
He's a man of our times,
With a strength of right behind him,
And the wisdom to steer our ship of state,
For today,
From its oceans to its orchards,
From its cities to his mountains,
You have a voice, you have a choice
For a man called Duryea.

But his greatest love was politics,
Like his father loved before him,
He left his boat for Albany,
Some twenty years of late,
Now he's runnin' there for Governor,
With his record out before him,
He's a leader of the people
That helped build...
The Empire State.

CHORUS
He's a man of our times,
With a strength of right behind him,
And the wisdom to steer our ship of state,
For today,
From its ocean to its orchards,
From its cities to his mountains,
You have a voice, you have a choice
For a man called Duryea.

*   *   *

Chris Johnson is home from the campaign trail now. He has been on the road, living in a trailor, for over a month. During that time, campaigning for the man he believed in, he logged 3,300 miles and visited virtually every city and town in the State of New York. He has come home exhausted, drained, and not just a little depressed about the defeat of his neighbor, Perry B. Duryea of Montauk, in the run for the governorship.

"I still say he'd have made a damn good governor," Johnson said over the phone.

"Why don't you come over? Have a drink and watch the sunset." I asked.

"I'd love it."

"Be there about four. It sets at an ungodly hour these days."

* * *

Even at four o'clock, the temperature was in the high fifties. It was a rare, early November afternoon, the sky was clear, and the sun was bright, and so we sat in deck chairs, outside, watching the sun go down over Three Mile Harbor. We ate pretzels and drank cheap French wine.

"You know what was surprising," Chris said, "White Plains. They've done terrific things with White Plains. You watch it. It's going to be the City of the Future."

"Yeah?"

"And Buffalo. That's a pretty underrated city, Buffalo. Ever been to Buffalo?"

"Not since I was eleven. They had trollies in Buffalo when I was eleven."

"Well, if you ever get up to Buffalo, you've got to eat at a restaurant called the Cloisters. What a place that is. The food is magnificent, the ambiance is like antiques. In fact, it IS antiques. The Cloisters Restaurant is sort of a junk shop with delicious food."

We sipped our wine for awhile, and we watched the sun set lower in the sky. As we did, Chris talked more and more about his experience on the campaign trail. I was fascinated by it, and

179

encouraged him. How often is it that a friend drives for a month around the state playing his guitar and living in a trailer?

"It was really something I wanted to do," Chris said. "Somehow, you know, I wanted to have an effect on this election, I wanted to have my convictions help the man I believed in. And what better way? This was not some slick TV commercial, or some public relations man's idea. We were real people, and we were entertaining and reaching out to the real people in the state. It was an old-fashioned kind of campaigning. The kind they don't do any more. And I think I made a difference. We sure made a lot of friends and handed out lots of literature."

"How did it work? Did you just drive up, park and play?"

"Well, pretty much. We had this old mail truck that used to belong to Henry Mund. And we would go wherever the campaign people thought it would be best for us to go. Then we would park and set up. Mostly, we set up in shopping centers. God, I think I've played in the parking lot of every shopping center in the State of New York. It was a sea of cars. Let me tell you. If cars could vote, Perry would be Governor. I must have sung and played to a million cars."

"Did you live in the mail truck?"

"No, no. We had a big Winnebago trailor that went around with the mail truck. And I lived in that. It was me, Dick Blake who drove the mail truck, and Kit O'Brien who drove the Winnebago. That was it. And you know? We had an awful lot of good times. It was really a lot of fun, even if Perry lost. One time, I remember, we were up in Rochester and were told to go down to this big outdoor market near the railroad tracks and set up around ten o'clock in the morning. This was the big wholesale market, where all the merchants in town would come to buy their fresh produce for the day. Anyway, we set up there next to a little restaurant called the Athens Restaurant, and after awhile, Pat Moynihan came out. He's a pretty well-known Democrat, as you know, and as it happened, he was inside the restaurant with a local television crew, filming his endorsement for Carey. What the problem was, was that we were singing too loud. There he was, inside, talking for Carey. But all the TV people could pick up was my song for Perry B. Duryea. I have another Duryea song to the tune of WABASH CANNON-BALL. It can be pretty loud. So he came out and asked very politely if we could turn it down or go somewhere else, and we very politely declined. Eventually, Moynihan gave up. But it was all in good humor."

"What else happened?"

"Oh, lots of things. One time, I remember, we were up in Utica, and there was a guy taking a poll with us. This was one of the funniest things. This pollster was very concerned about the lack of interest in the election, and he kept asking people to what did they attribute this lack of interest. 'Do you think it is ignorance or apathy?' he asked this one fellow. 'I don't know, and I don't care,' the fellow replied."

"That's pretty funny."

"Something else that was funny. We collected campaign stickers and pasted them all over the mail truck. We had campaign stickers from just about every Republican running in the State of New York. And I remember one of them that read JOHN SICK RECEIVER OF TAXES. He was running in the Salina District of Syracuse. And he won, I think. I've saved

181

the sticker, because it's a classic. I'll show it to you sometime. And I met Mr. Sick. A very nice fellow."

"Amazing."

"You know, there was only one thing we really needed whenever we came into a town. Our show was really self-contained. We'd fold down the stage and all, but then we had to find an outlet for electricity. And this wasn't so easy as you might think. First of all, we'd play on a Sunday somewhere and have to find a grocery store or something that would be open. Then we'd have to find out that he was a Republican and would be willing to make a small donation of his electricity for the afternoon just for the cause. Other times, when nobody was around, we'd just have to find a place to hook up. I remember one in Albany once, we ran our wire into the lobby of a twelve-story office building and found an outlet. We'd hooked up and were just getting underway, when all of a sudden our plug and wire came flying out of the building, followed by a very angry bureaucrat. 'Who do you think you are?' he yelled, standing in front of this twelve-story building. 'This is my building, and I'm in charge of it, You can't just come in and steal electricity just like that!' Undoubtedly a Democrat."

"Did you ever get tired of campaigning?"

"Oh boy, did I. Once, it was late in the day, and I had been playing all day, and off we were supposed to go to a cocktail party for candidate Leonard Berson in the Italian section of North Syracuse. I'd had it. I told the others to go, just hand out literature, but I was going to take the Winnebago and somehow, just find myself a quiet place somewhere. Well, the others went off in the mail truck and, looking around, through some buildings and trees, I could just make out a chink of blue that

182

was the water of Lake Onondaga there in Syracuse. It was late in the day. There'd be a sunset. And so, without any idea of what roads to take, I just drove toward it. I went through yards, parking lots, over a knocked-down chain link fence, up an embankment, across some railroad tracks, down the embankment, sideways across a four-lane highway, and finally got to the shore. It was a beautiful sunset, much like tonight's, and when I got there, having crossed all these obstacles and encumbrances, I got out of the car and just raised my arms to the water and sunset. You know on TV that commercial where the Indian raises his arms and a tear rolls down his cheek as he ponders on what man has done to the environment? Well, that is how I felt just then. There was just me, the water, the land and the sunset. And there had been all these parking lots, yards, fences, highways and other junk that had been placed in the way. Oh well."

The sun had set now, a brilliant ball of fire over the woods of Northwest on the other side of the harbor. A chill had come over the evening now, a brisk November chill.

"Enough of this," I said. "Come on in. I'll build a fire."

Crutchley's Crullers

At three o'clock in the afternoon, the phone rang.

"Hello, Crutchley's."

"Crutchley's Bakery? This is the Dallas Opera House calling. We'd like to place an order for one gross of cruller hearts. Can you ship them in time for our reception a week from Friday?"

"Of course we can," Lydia Crutchley said.

Lydia stood in her apron, covered with a white dusting of powdered sugar, in the front room of Crutchley's Bakery store on Hampton Road, Southampton. In the back room, Fenton Crutchley bent forward, watching the cruller hearts cook in the fryer. Cruller hearts were the only product in the Crutchley bakery.

An order of crullers from Dallas was nothing new to the Crutchleys. Over the fifty-one years that the Crutchleys ran their bakery, orders for cruller hearts came from all over the world. There were telephone orders from California, from Vietnam, even Antartica for this single most remarkable product.

Once, the niece of Fenton Crutchley was introduced to Edmund Land, the photography genius, in a town in upstate New York. This niece had always wanted to meet Mr. Land, the inventor of the Polaroid camera, and she told him so.

"If your name is Crutchley," Mr. Land said, "then I'm excited to meet YOU. Perhaps you could get me some of those famous cruller hearts your uncle makes in Southampton. Or perhaps you could at least get me a letter of introduction. I've been unsuccessful in obtaining the cruller hearts lately."

As the fame of these remarkable cruller hearts

grew, indeed it became more difficult to obtain them. For regardless of the demand, Fenton Crutchley, covered with the same sugar dust as his wife, never exceeded the output he felt comfortable with: one hundred dozen a day in winter, two hundred dozen a day in summer. Long ago, the Crutchleys took their store sign off the street. People who knew about them took up all their production. They couldn't produce any more.

Beginning in the late 1920's, the Crutchleys mailed out approximately three thousand boxes of cruller hearts every year. Young men at college would receive them from their parents. When the young men got married, boxes would be sent to their children. When these children grew up and married, boxes would be sent to their children. And by 1978, the year before the Crutchleys closed their bakery, there were cases where four generations had been receiving care packages of cruller hearts.

In the late 1940's, a man approached Gary Cooper in a cafe in Rome.

"The last time I saw you was in Crutchley's," the man said.

Gary Cooper took this total stranger out on the town.

It is true that Fenton Crutchley, now in his 69th year, could have sold his business and had it continued.

"I would rather let the business go down the drain," he told me on the last day the shop was open, "than let someone take over the name and put out an inferior product."

"This is terrible," an older woman said to Lydia Crutchley that last day. "When I think of all the people...." There were tears in her eyes.

"We couldn't notify all the customers," Lydia said.

One day in the early 1950's, the fryer which cooks

185

the cruller hearts broke down for a total of three hours. Chaos resulted among the customers and the incident made front page news in the Southampton Press.

*   *   *

Dear Mr. and Mrs. Crutchley:

I just want to say hi and tell you how I am. When Mrs. Alverez sent me hearts at school (boarding school) it was a big hit. Nobody knew what they were. Right now I have a 24-box on my desk.

Chris Gaynor
Vancouver, BC

Crutchley's cruller hearts are small spheres of doughnuts, about one inch in diameter. Lydia Crutchley packages them in clear plastic bags of 16 and 32, either shaken up with powdered white sugar, plain, or plain with a small bag of sugar on the side for dipping. The plastic bag, tied at the top, was then placed in a white plastic box with the green imprint "Crutchley's" on the side.

Here is the recipe for Crutchley's famous cruller hearts.

Mr. Crutchley's Crullers

   1 cup sugar
   2 large eggs, chilled
   1 egg yolk, chilled
   1½ teaspoons salt
   ½ cup chilled evaporated milk
   ½ cup ice water
   3 teaspoons vanilla
   4 cups patent flour [not cake or pastry flour]
   4 teaspoons non-alum baking powder [see note]
   2 teaspoons freshly ground nutmeg
   4 tablespoons melted shortening

Shortening for deep frying
Confectioner's sugar for dusting

1. Using a heavy-duty mixer, combine sugar, eggs and salt and beat on high speed until creamy, about two minutes.

2. Add milk, ice water and vanilla, and, on low speed, gradually add sifted flour, baking powder, nutmeg.

3. Add melted shortening [not too hot] and mix at low speed until thoroughly blended.

4. Chill batter in refrigerator for eight hours.

5. Knead dough until pliable, four to five minutes. Roll out [not too thin, just under half an inch] and cut with a regular doughnut cutter or the smaller heart cutter. Re-roll dough, using as little flour as possible. Cut remainder.

6. Fry in deep fat between 375 and 380 degrees until brown all over.

7. Drain on cooling rack to room temperature and dust with confectioner's sugar to taste.

Yield: 4 dozen regular doughnuts or about 128 hearts.

Note: A baking powder without alum is best, but if you can't get it, use regular baking powder which, unfortunately, imparts a slight metallic taste to the crullers.

Terrors of a Rural Boxholder

Up until quite recently, I was one of those people who went down to the Post Office to get his mail. I would come into the lobby, jiggle the combination on my post office box, and take out the few letters the postmen had put in from the other side. Then I would spend the next ten minutes chatting with whatever people I would find at the Post Office at that time. It was a nice social occasion.

Last spring, however, I moved into a house on Three Mile Harbor Road in East Hampton, and along with it, out on the street, came an official rural mailbox from which, I was told, I would henceforth be receiving my mail. I thought I would miss the little coffee klaches at the Post Office, but on the other hand, I had been doing that for almost twenty years on the East End, and so now perhaps it was time for something new. I really looked forward to the first day when I would see the little red flag on the side of the mailbox sticking straight up. This, I was told, would be the signal that there was mail inside that needed to be picked up.

*   *   *

Three days after we moved into this little house, a policeman knocked on the back door.

"Is this your mailbox?" he asked.

He held up a piece of shredded and twisted black metal.

"Yes, that's it. What happened?"

"Fellow smashed into it with his car. Joy riding. We got him though. He knocked down about four mailboxes on the street before we caught up with

188

him."

"That's terrible."

"Sure is. We've got him downtown. Care to press charges?"

"Over a mailbox? Is it necessary?"

"No. We've got other property owners who are pressing charge. Well, anyway, I just needed to confirm that this was your mailbox."

He handed the shredded mailbox to me.

"What about my mail?" I asked.

"I don't know anything about that. But if you'd like to press charges you could probably make a claim and get a settlement for your mailbox."

"Thanks."

The officer left. And without the mailbox out on the street, the house seemed rather cut off. There was no place to put the mail.

The following day, I went to the Village Hardware Store on Newtown Lane, and for about eleven dollars bought a brand new regulation rural mailbox. It was disassembled and came in pieces with nuts and bolts and screws, but I figured I could put the thing together. Back at the house, I spent about an hour on it, then carted it outside and put it where the old one had been. I looked at it. Sitting on its little post, it was right about the height where a mailman could lean out of his car window, open the

front, and put in the mail. But if was also right there on the road just two feet off the pavement itself. If the last one got hit, then this one could too. Looking around, I saw that I could move the mailbox up the driveway about eight feet. The postman could still get at it, although now he'd have to swerve a bit to do it. But it would be well out of the way of drunks and joyriders. I moved it.

On the fourth day, however, I got a telephone call from a relative in another part of East Hampton.

"We have a letter here for you," they said. "They delivered it to Harbor View Lane by mistake."

"That's funny."

"It sure is. It's addressed to Dan Rattiner, 26 Three Mile Harbor Road. Don't you have a mailbox?"

"I sure do."

I picked up this letter the next day, and it was not very important. But it seemed odd the local post office would deliver a letter clearly addressed to Three Mile Harbor Road to Harbor View Lane.

I called the East Hampton Post Office. And they said they would look into it.

Four days later, a message was taped to the BACK door of our house. It was from the postman, and it said that our post office mailbox was too far off the road and was an inconvenience for the driver, and they would not deliver my mail until I had it moved back to where it was before. This note was delivered by the postman, who drove up the driveway past the mailbox, around to the back of the house and then to the back door. The mailbox apparently had some contagious disease.

Anyway, I moved the mailbox back to its old position. I would brave the joyriders. But a week went by and STILL there was no mail.

190

Then, on the eighth day, all sorts of things happened. Another phone call came from Harbor View Lane with the information that a letter had again been delivered there. A phone call also came from a friend in New York City saying that his letter to me had been returned marked UNKOWN. Wasn't I living at 26 Three Mile Harbor Road?

About three in the afternoon came the killer.

"Hello? Mr. Rattiner? This is the Long Island Lighting Company calling. I'm sorry, but I have to inform you that since you have not been paying your bill, we will turn your power out at noon Wednesday."

"Bill? Bill?"

The Lighting Company, it turned out, had been sending me a bill, and that, too, had been returned marked UNKNOWN. And it too had been addressed to me at 26 Three Mile Harbor Road. By a computer, even.

"I'll look into this," I told the Lighting Company.

"We'll give you seventy-two hours," the Lighting Company said cheerfully.

*   *   *

At this point, there was nothing further to do than to get down to it with the East Hampton Post Office.

"You do not live at 26 Three Mile Harbor Road," an official told me.

"Yes, I do."

"There IS no 26 Three Mile Harbor Road. The numbers start down at the corner of Main Street, go up into the hundreds, and then end about two hundred yards before they get to your house. There is an empty lot at 26 Three Mile Harbor Road."

"What are you talking about?"

"Up where you live, the road continues on, but it goes by another name. Two hundred yards before

191

your house, it becomes THREE MILE HARBOR HOG CREEK ROAD. The numbers go back to zero, and they go on up for a second time. Your address is 26 Three Mile Harbor Hog Creek Road."

This was the craziest thing I ever heard of. The road for its entire length, both south of my house and north of my house, has been known from time immemorial as Three Mile Harbor Road. It is so listed on all roadmaps.

"My deed says 26 Three Mile Harbor Road."

"Your deed is wrong."

"The restaurants who have ads in my paper say Three Mile Harbor Road."

"The restaurants are wrong."

"For God's Sake, it's common knowledge."

"Common knowledge is wrong. Go look at the street signs."

I went and looked at the street signs. They had another opinion. The street signs have two names on them. "Three Mile Harbor Road" appears on a upper row. "Hog Creek Road" appears on a lower row. It is a very great deal to read on one street sign.

I returned with this information to the Post Office.

"The street signs are wrong."

But you know, when all is said and done, there is one thing the post office has that overrides all other considerations in this matter. They have your mail.

*   *   *

And so, what I have done to get my mail is I've informed every person I can think of of my new address. The computer at the Long Island Lighting Company happily spits out letters addressed:

26 3 Mi Hrbr Hog Crk Rd.

My friends joyously write to me at 26 Three Mile Harbor Hog Creek Road. My creditors send me bills at 26 Three Mile Harbor Hog Creek Road. And I've even made up personal stationery that says 26 Three Mile Harbor Hog Creek Road.

But I still don't understand it.

*   *   *

This morning, I got a letter addressed to a Mr. Stuart. I do not know a Mr. Stuart, but there it was in my official rural mailbox. (The mailman, by the way does not stick up the red flag). The letter was addressed to "Mr. Stuart, Box 26, Three Mile Harbor Road, East Hampton."

And I've been wondering what I could do with Mr. Stuart's letter. The easiest thing, of course, would be to bring it back to the East Hampton Post Office. However, the letter looks too important to entrust to the East Hampton Post Office.

Instead, what I'd like to do is direct a personal appeal to Mr. Stuart or to anyone who knows Mr. Stuart at Box 26 Three Mile Harbor Road. Mr. Stuart, if you would like your letter, you are welcome to give me a call, anytime, either at home or here at Dan's Papers. We could set up a meeting at some mutually convenient spot, and I'd be happy to deliver you your letter safe and sound.

Preservation of Springs

The year was 2173, and the large, all-window tourist bus was silently gliding along the streets of Springs. The streets were deserted, and there wasn't a soul to be seen in any direction.

"So here we are, ladies and gentlemen," the tourist guide said, "entering the most famous artist's colony the world has ever seen."

"What's that over there?" a fat woman with sunglasses asked.

"That's the studio of Harlan Jackson."

"THE Harlan Jackson?"

"That's right. The man with all the famous paintings in the Louvre. On the second floor, where he actually did all his paintings, Mr. Jackson's brushes and easels are all carefully preserved just as he used them."

"Gee," a tall man in a Hawaiian sport shirt said.

"Now, almost directly in front of us is ANOTHER studio, that of sculptor Tino Nivola. He's the man, for those of you who don't now, who designed the two-thousand-foot sculpture out in front of the New United Nations Building in Chicago."

"Who didn't know THAT," the fat woman said.

"I always thought his name was pronounced NIVOLI," another woman said, "like in the Italian."

"Now we're passing some other studios, restored to just as they were when the famous artists last used them. On the left is the studio of Herman Cherry, the first American artist to make over ten million dollars selling his own paintings during his lifetime. And on the right is the studio of Lunchtime

O'Booze.''

"Lunchtime O'Booze?'' the fat lady wanted to know.

"Well, he's not quite as famous as all the others,'' the guide said, "but he did paint the ceiling in the lobby of the Metropolitan Museum of Art. Of course, they caught him at it and threw him out.''

"How many famous artists had their studios in the Springs?'' the fat lady asked.

"Every single studio here in the Springs,'' the guide said, "was at one time or another the home of a famous artist or sculptor. And they've all been preserved. Nearly 400 in all.''

The bus made a left turn, and then slowly came to a stop in front of a house in the woods.

"Now here's our first stop,'' the guide said. "You can leave your souvenir items on your seats if you want to as you get out.'' The tourists got up and looked at each other questioningly. "Don't worry,'' the guide said. "This isn't the City. Things are perfectly safe.''

The tourists, all fifty-five of them, slowly got out of the bus and lined up behind the guide. They walked up the path, looking cautiously left and right.

"Stay on the path,'' the guide says. "Don't walk on the grass or touch anything, please.''

"Gosh,'' the fat woman said.

195

The procession walked through the woods and into a studio a considerable distance from the road. The main space was roped off with a maroon velvet chain, similar to the ones they have in theatre lobbies.

"This is the studio of Jim Brooks," the guide said matter-of-factly. "As you can see, all the paint cans have been left out with their tops off, just as Mr. Brooks used to leave them.

"How do the paints keep their color?" a man with a Japanese camera wanted to know.

"Well, they DO fade," the guide said. "But every fifty years or so, the colors are retouched."

The tour walked further along through the woods toward the studio of Charlotte Parks. Other than the sound of a soft breeze and the clicking of camera shutters, there wasn't a sound at all.

"It's so PEACEFUL here," the fat lady said. "No WONDER they got so many wonderful paintings done."

"WHAT IS THAT?" someone shouted, and the whole procession stopped. There, off to the left of the path was a tall, and very dark brown horse, standing completely still and staring at the tourist party.

"That is a HORSE," the guide said. "Don't worry, it is completely stuffed. It's simply been placed here by the staff so you can see some of the things these famous painters worked with as models."

"Are there any Bonackers?" the fat lady wanted to know.

"Oh yes, the Bonackers, the local people. Of course, there are. There is a complete plaster display of three Bonackers, knee-deep in Three Mile Harbor, hauling in a net full of fish. It is quite a display."

"Gee," the fat lady said.

They continued their walk and arrived at the studio of Charlotte Parks, not far away.

"As you can see, we have left Miss Parks' skylight exactly as it was. And there is her space heater and her shawl."

"My goodness, Charlotte Parks' shawl. Her famous shawl," the fat lady said.

They returned to the bus. They drove up the Springs-Fireplace Road and passed the restored Aşhawagh Hall, where a display of copies of Jackson Pollack's paintings were hung.

"Of course, none of the originals are here in Springs anymore," the guide was saying, "they're much too important. The closest Pollack is in New York. Now, if you'll look down this street, past the wooden ducks in the pond, you'll get a glimpse of the famous 'Miller General Store' where many of these famous painters bought their groceries."

"Wasn't that the Mr. Miller who became chairman of the board of U.S. Steel?" someone wanted to know.

"Mr. Miller was a very generous man," the guide said, "and in the early years, when one of these artists was poor, Mr. Miller often traded his groceries for their paintings. Yes, he is the man who wound up chairman of the board of U.S. Steel. But you've got to remember, those paintings might have wound up being worthless, too. Mr. Miller took a gamble on that."

The bus moved down the road, and the guide pointed out the studios of V.V. Rankin, Hedda Stern, Lee Krasner and Ibram Lassaw. Then it arrived and stopped at a low, unimposing one-story wooden building by the side of the road.

"And this is the famous 'Vinnie's Place'," the

guide said, "left just as it was when the artists used to come here to play pool and pass the time. Now be careful not to touch anything."

The tour group made their way through the modest front doors and into the bar, where groups in bronze had been sculpted sitting around various tables. There were hamburgers and French fried potatoes and ketchup and beer, all carefully reproduced in plastic.

"As many as a hundred famous artists sat in this bar," the guide said.

"At one time?"

"At one time."

"What about the ceiling?"

"Oh yes," the guide said, "another job by Lunchtime O'Booze. You can see that it's standing up pretty well, considering it is done in Crayolas." They all stood there, looking up at the ceiling. "Nobody's quite figured out what it means just yet," the guide said.

They all took some pictures then went back to the bus to visit some more studios. And two hours later, exhausted from having seen another forty of fifty, they arrived at the Springs entry gate where they had originally paid their admission fee.

"Before the bus returns you all to downtown East Hampton," the guide said, "I would like to present each and every one of you with a special gift — an actual full-size scale model of a can of Campbell's Pork and Beans — exactly the same as the ones Mr. Miller used to trade for famous paintings."

"Gosh," said the big fat lady.

"Gee," said the man with the Hawaiian shirt.

The bus passed through the entry gate, past the big sign reading VILLAGE OF SPRINGS, HISTORICAL SITE, and back into the City of East Hampton.

Traffic was backed up in every direction. The telephone company was digging up one part of the street, the power company another. Next to the forty-story Dan's Papers buiding, cars honked as they waited to get around the old Hook Mill, clearly obstructing the road for so many years. The bus pulled off into an underground tunnel where the air conditioning was still functioning and the smog was less thick, and there the tourists disembarked to make their way back outside to hail their taxis, still clutching their scale model cans of Campbell's Pork and Beans.

Warlock's Halloween

The warlocks arrived in Montauk on a Friday. There were six of them, as near as anybody can remember, and they came with the tools of their trade: shovels for digging shallow graves, gasoline for rings of fire, wooden crosses and drums. They also had a large tent with them as it was their intention to camp out in the woods of Montauk for three days, celebrate Halloween in their own ritualistic way, and then return from whence they came.

The warlocks drove through town in a perfectly ordinary looking station wagon, headed out toward the Montauk Lighthouse, and then turned right on a dirt road opposite the Deep Hollow Ranch. They passed Andy Warhol's house, which was not occupied that afternoon. They continued on for nearly a mile and a half past Warhol's house until they arrived at a large, ten-acre piece of vacant land between the Peter Beard estate and Roger McCanns house. Here, deep in a woods beside a clearing, they made their camp. They were less than five hundred yards from the sea. And they were within sight of the Montauk Lighthouse.

Roger McCann and Gladys Little remember the warlocks quite clearly. The six of them, some women but mostly men, had knocked at their door that first evening to ask if they could fill their empty bottles with water.

"We're living in a tent just through the woods," one of them told Roger McCann. "We've rented the site for the weekend. But we have no water and would appreciate it if we could use your outdoor faucet."

Roger saw no reason why they could not. The visitors seemed pleasant enough, although they were a little strange. Roger remembers that they were all very thin and ascetic looking. They were dressed in rough clothes, but with beads and chains which made them appear to be city people. And what the hell. Andy Warhol's house was just down the street. All sorts of unusual people had been tramping about.

"By the way," one of them said, "if you hear any unusual noises, it is just us. We'll be celebrating Halloween."

Now what did they mean by that? Roger wondered. Nobody had told him they were warlocks.

*   *   *

The next few days went by uneventfully, and there wasn't anybody who knew what the warlocks were doing in those woods. Roger McCann and Gladys Little went to several Halloween parties during that time. There was one at the Shagwong, and several others in private homes. But at no time did they see any of the six aesthetic looking visitors who were camped out in the woods. The visitors were apparently keeping to themselves.

Monday was October thirty-first. It was a clear, blue autumn day, and since the majority of the tourists had gone home for the week, it was certain to be a quiet one. For the most part, Halloween in Montauk had been celebrated during the weekend before.

But Roger McCann was curious to note that the visitors had not gone home that day. If anything, their activity in the woods next door was even more intense, as if it were leading up to some sort of climax.

One of the visitors came by for even more water

that afternoon, and they were sociable enough. Whatever it was, it was none of Roger's and Gladys's business after all.

*   *   *

Roger McCann and Gladys Little went to bed rather early that Monday night. The weekend was over, and the pair were tired. Roger was particularly eager to get an early start on the repairs for his fishing boat the following morning.

At three a.m., however, there were some very strange sounds outside. There were chanting sounds and drumming sounds, and the noise awoke both Roger and Gladys. Gladys went to a window.

"There is some sort of fire out there," she said.

Roger joined her and could see the flickering of a bonfire through the woods.

"It's Halloween," Roger said. "Remember? Those people said there would be some sort of ritual."

"I wonder what it is?" Gladys thought.

The chanting and drumming got louder. There were no words that could be made out, just eerie wailing and moaning noises.

"It sounds almost like an Indian war dance," Gladys said.

"It sure does."

"Do you want to go see?"

"What?"

"Why don't we tiptoe over and just peer through the bushes?"

Roger thought about this. "You can go if you want. But I'm going back to bed. It's just some crazy thing, if you ask me."

Gladys thought about this and then decided that if Roger wouldn't go, she wouldn't either. No sense going out in the middle of the night all alone.

*   *   *

The following morning, the warlocks were gone. Roger and Gladys walked around the property and found the remains of several large fireworks beside Peter Beard's mill. They also found that an old wrecked rowboat that belonged to the Beards was missing.

"Why would they want that?" Roger wondered. "The whole bottom of it is eaten out. It couldn't go anywhere."

There were other unusual things. The tent that had been used, for example, was still in place. It had been a perfectly good tent, yet it had been left behind. Why?

In another part of the woods, there was a clearing. Here, clearly burned in the ground was a singed circle about twenty feet in diameter. Without a doubt, it had been a ring of fire. And without a doubt, it had burned on Halloween evening.

Most unusual of all were the graves. In another part of the woods, Roger and Gladys found eight freshly dug graves with the remains of a bonfire nearby. The graves had been filled in, but there was no doubt that is what they were. They were about seven feet long and three feet wide, and they had been dug in two rows of four. What part had these graves played in the rituals of Halloween evening?

For some reason, it never occurred to Roger McCann or Gladys Little to report the whole thing to the police. It had been Halloween evening, after all, and no permanent damage, other than the loss of a worthless boat, had been done. Furthermore, the visitors had gone without a trace. There was no one there to talk to, no one in interrogate. And certainly stranger things had happened in Montauk from time to time.

*   *   *

It was not until last week, almost nine months later, that the police came to investigate. Oddly, it had been a member of the Yonkers Police Department who had turned in the call. This Yonkers policeman had heard a rumor that there were eight shallow graves located near Montauk Point, and so he called the East Hampton force and asked them to investigate.

East Hampton police officers, complete with spades and shovels, turned up at the McGann house on a Friday. Could they be shown where the graves were located? Certainly they could. Gingerly, the police officers walked over to the woods where the graves were still quite fresh, and slowly they began to dig.

"If you hit something hard, stop," one of them said.

They dug, but they found nothing. Whatever it was that the warlocks had buried in the graves, they had taken with them when they left.

"Perhaps they lay in these shallow graves themselves," one of the policemen suggested. "That would be part of the warlocks' Halloween ceremony, as I understand it."

"Perhaps," Roger said.

The police left. The old broken rowboat, it turned out, was one and a half miles away, on the beach at the foot of the cliff. McGann and a young friend of his tried to haul it back, but they couldn't get it up the cliff. It remains at the foot of the cliff today.

The tent remains in the woods today, too. It is in tatters now, and one of the ridge poles has fallen. But it still marks the site where, nine months ago, some warlocks conducted their Halloween rituals in the woods near Montauk Point.

Superbowl XV
In The
Hamptons

Over 70,000,000 people watched the Superbowl on Sunday, January 18. This was more than watched Armstrong take his first steps on the moon. In fact, it was more than had ever watched one single event in the history of television.

One of those people who watched this football game was a heavyset man who lives in Sag Harbor, Long Island. At ten minutes to two, he finished his lunch, got up from the kitchen table where his wife and children were still sitting, and walked into the living room. He wiped his mouth on his sleeve. Then he flicked on the television with his remote tuner and sat down on the living room sofa.

"Bring me a beer, would you?" he shouted into the kitchen.

"What the hell are you doing?" his wife answered.

"What do you mean, what am I doing? It's the Superbowl."

On the television, the sound came on, then the picture. Tommy Brookshier was talking to the coach of the Dallas Cowboys, and both he and the coach were green. The man got up and adjusted the color.

The wife walked into the living room, her hands on her hips.

"You said you were going to take the screens

down today."

"Look. Pittsburgh is playing Dallas. Do you mind?"

"Do I mind? Do I mind? It's the middle of January and the screens are still on all the windows."

"Then get one of the children to do it."

"One of our daughters?"

"Then do it yourself. Can't a man have any peace and quiet in his own home? The kickoff is in ten minutes."

The wife walked back into the kitchen, and then made a decision that would shortly affect parts of Sag Harbor and Bridgehampton for the rest of the afternoon.

"Will you get me a beer goddammit?"

The woman did not answer. She was in the back hall putting on her hat and coat, clattering around.

"Where are you going?" the man yelled from the living room.

"Out."

"Well, good for you."

There were more noises in the back hall. Then the door closed, and the man could hear his wife out in the garage walking around the car. The walls were thin. Clearly, he heard her removing the shotgun from its rack over the workbench. Then he heard her get into the car.

Pat Summerall was busy talking to Terry Hanratty, the backup quarterback for the Pittsburgh Steelers. Would Hanratty play if Terry Bradshaw's knee was reinjured?

"Well, that would be up to Coach Knox," Hanratty said. "But if he wants me in there, of course I'll give it all I've got."

Tires squealed, and the man heard his wife backing the car recklessly out of the driveway.

"Go kill yourself!" he shouted after her. What in hell did she want with a gun anyway?

On the screen, some cheerleaders were tossing flaming batons high into the sky. There was the Goodyear blimp.

"We'll be right back with more of the opening festivities of the Superbowl here in Miami in just a few minutes," an announcer said.

*   *   *

The above incident may, or may not have happened. It does appear extremely likely to have happened, however, in the light of events. What did happen throughout the Hamptons at exactly 2:03 in the afternoon was that the Pittsburgh Steelers kicked off to the Dallas Cowboys. A vast majority of the population of the Hamptons was inside, facing their television sets, watching Golden Richards field the ball and begin to run it back. In fact, most of the police officers in the area, sitting in their station houses, were watching small black and white portables, ready to break away if something important were to happen in the area. It would have to be pretty important, however.

At 2:05, the teams lined up almost at midfield for the first play of the game. It had been a good kickoff runback, with a lateral and a reversal that had caught the Pittsburgh team completely flatfooted. They would have a tough time with the football where it was, and they would have to dig in.

The crowd roared as the ball was hiked for the first play. A Dallas halfback skittered off tackle and made a yard or two. Not much. The team met in a huddle in back of the line, and the quarterback, Roger Staubach, called the second play. Another run and another few yards. And then, as the men were trotting back for the huddle for the third time, virtually all the television sets in parts of Sag Harbor and Bridgehampton went flooey. There was nothing but white snow. A sign that somehow, somewhere, the signal had gone dead.

People leaped up from their chairs and began frantically adjusting the dials in front of them. Nothing happened. They tried different channels, and they got more snow. No Superbowl. Something was wrong with the cablevision.

By way of explanation, it should be noted this area of eastern Long Island is too remote from New York City to pick up the New York stations. Without a tall, expensive aerial, or without a line of the local cablevision hookup, all the people of the Hamptons can receive is a lethargic Connecticut television station known as Channel 8. This station features old reruns of the Price is Right and Truth or Consequences. At 2 o'clock in the afternoon of January 18, it was showing an old western. Everyone began to go berserk.

Telephone calls lit up the police stations around the area. The local company, Long Island Cablevision, which services about half the sets in the area, was swamped with phone calls.

Channel 8 was loud and clear. Obviously, it had to be the cablevision. What had happened? What had gone wrong at the tower?

Nobody at the Cablevision office knew. There was, in fact, just one person in the office that Sunday afternoon taking care of things. That person was a secretary. Everyone else was home watching the Superbowl on the cable.

In all the Hamptons, there are maybe sixty people who could watch the Superbowl without the cablevision. These people, all of them wealthy, had years ago installed fifty foot television towers adjacent to their homes. They had not known that cablevision would ever come into the area. And they were not going to wait around. For a few hundred dollars, at that time, they could put up a tower of their own. It was a luxury, but they could afford it, and so they did. Now, in the middle of the middle of the third play of Superbowl XV, their telephones began to jump off the wall. The calls were from friends, and friends of friends, and long lost brothers-in-law. Could they come over? The game was just starting. They'd bring their own chips and beer.

Beginning about 2:15, crowds of automobiles dashed frantically, and at high speed, over the various roads of the Hamptons. This continued for nearly a half hour until those lucky enough to know rich friends with TV towers had got themselves resettled.

For the rest, it was wait and see. One could have faith that the problems of the cablevision would be shortly restored. In the meantime, it would be the old western movie and, surprise of surprises, old fashioned conversation.

The first half went by, and then the third quarter. About ten minutes after the game had ended, some repairmen from the Long Island Lighting Company, working in the woods at the site of the cablevision tower, came upon the trouble.

"Look here," said one of the workmen.

The second repairman, who had been busy checking the wiring that threaded into the tower itself, walked over. It was a cold day, bitter cold at 5 degrees, with a biting wind. He walked down the short path, through some dried leaves, to the transformers adjacent to the tower.

"Shotgun blast," the first workman said waving a

gloved hand.

There were three of them, and they had hit the bullseye. The transformer was dead.

"Who would do a crazy thing like that?"

* * *

In every way, the Superbowl was an American event. It was the biggest spectacular ever to be seen on television. A TV commercial cost $230,000, which was to be a record. Over a million words and pictures were written about the event by 1,735 newspapermen and commentators. A record number of private aircraft, over 50, landed at the nearby Opa-Locka Airport. Meanwhile, the commercial airlines had put on a record 98 extra flights to bring the people into Miami.

Executives from every major corporation attended Superbowl XV. People from Ford, Chrysler, Coca-Cola, American Express and Zenith filled up the hotel rooms. Lincoln-Mercury even hired a cruise ship, the Monarch Sun, to take 600 Lincoln-Mercury salesmen and their wives on a quick trip to the Bahamas just prior to the game. It was a good tax write-off.

Almost everyone saw the game. In parts of Sag Harbor and Bridgehampton, however, the game was a television catastrophe of the first order, as the event above was reported in the local papers.

Only one person was very, very happy about it out there. Our guess is that is was a woman.

Hampton Light and Power Company

Four years ago, when the Arabs raised their oil prices, the people of the Hamptons were as upset as anyone else. Unlike everyone else, however, the people here actually DID something about it. They formed the Hampton Light and Power Company, funded it with ten million dollars in taxpayers' money, and today they are totally self-sufficient.

"Our energy costs are not low," said Adam Harrison, the manager of Hampton Light and Power. "But these costs are our own. The Arabs can raise the price of oil as much as they want as far as we are concerned. It won't affect us in the slightest. We don't use a drop."

In fact, Hampton Light and Power runs on wind. Over a dozen windmills have been constructed in the last four years — the last one having been completed just six months ago — and these windmills provide all the electricity needed for heat and light from Westhampton Beach to Montauk Point.

"The Hamptons have a good deal of wind," Mr. Harrison said. "All we have done is take our fair share of it."

When the windmills were first proposed three and a half years ago, many local residents expressed their opposition on aesthetic grounds. Who wants to have ugly metal windmills sticking up in the sky throughout the area? This problem was solved though when the architects hired by Hampton Light and Power came up with an ingenious solution: Design all the windmills to look exactly like the old wooden windmills that dot

Holland and England. And that is exactly what was done.

"The tourists just love them," Mr. Harrison said.

Indeed, when the first of these beautiful new windmills was completed on the town green in East Hampton, it immediately became the showpiece of the town. Photographers took pictures of it, postcards came out bearing drawings of the mill. Even the East Hampton Village Police made a rendering of this windmill which they display today on the sides of all their police cars.

A second windmill was completed beside the Montauk Highway in Water Mill. And a third mill was constructed in a small park on Ocean Road in Bridgehampton.

"We followed the plans of the old English mills down to the very finest detail," Mr. Harrison said. "And we even constructed the mills out of old timbers and shingles. Only an expert could see that they are not three hundred years old."

More windmills were constructed. And before the power grid was finally completed in December of 1977, a total of thirteen mills were built in place. These provide enough power to service the entire needs of the Hamptons three hundred and sixty-five days of the year.

The transfer of authority from the Long Island Lighting Company took place on January 1, 1978. In an official ceremony, delayed for a day by a terrific snowstorm, Mayor Fred Erskine pushed the propeller of the first of the constructed windmills on East Hampton Town Green. It was an emotional moment. The High School band played, the lights in the town flickered for an instant, and then came on seemingly brighter than before. The system, as everyone had predicted it would, worked like a charm.

212

It took three days before all the towns converted to the Hampton Light and Power Company. But from that point until this, all the electrical and heating power in the area has come from these beautiful and, seemingly, very old windmills.

"It is not so much what is above ground that does the work," Mr. Harrison told us. "Below ground there are vast storage and supply areas. For instance, beneath the Hook Mill in East Hampton, there are four subbasements filled with storage batteries and support equipment. A permanent staff of seventeen works in these subbasements, living and taking their meals below the ground. Gathering the power from the wind — and then storing it — is no easy matter."

We asked Mr. Harrison why this storage facility could not have been built above the ground, and we got a very good answer.

"It was not aesthetically acceptable," he said. "How would it look, having an apparently three hundred year old windmill attached to a four story brick powerplant?"

Of course, not all of the old English windmills have four subbasements underneath them. Some have only two subbasements, and at least five of the windmills have no subbasements and no storage facilities at all.

"In these areas, which include North Sea, Hampton Bays and the Northwest Woods," Mr. Harrison said, "there are times when there is no power generated at all. But the people in these areas are aware of it. In fact, they voted for it and their bills are adjusted accordingly when they are without power on windless days."

It is for this reason that there are so many cookouts in North Sea, Hampton Bays and the Northwest Woods. It is just the local residents happily accommodating themselves between the windstorms.

Visitors from the City should take a lesson from the accomplishments of the Hampton Light and Power Company. When the blade of one windmill breaks, and the thing is out of service for a while, the power from the other windmills is transmitted through underground wires to make up for the loss — and the residents of the area with the broken windmill suffer no loss at all.

"It is the same principle as the northeast power grid," Mr. Harrison said. "When Big Allis in Queens breaks down, they just transfer the power from somewhere else."

It will be many years before the Hampton Light and Power Company can pay off the costs of the construction of the beautiful windmills and their storage facilities. But even for this autumn, Mr. Harrison and his board of directors are looking to expand the operation into other areas.

"If we get the big winds we usually get in the winter time," Mr. Harrison said, "we will be in a position to export some of our excess power. Connecticut Light and Power might want some. Con Ed might want some. And, of course, we will sell it all at current commercial rates, which are quite substantial."

Hampton L. and P. also intends to go into the bakery and knifesharpening business. By this time next year, as many as six retail stores will be established in the area selling bread and cakes that have been made from grain ground at the windmills.

"We will also sharpen kitchen knives at the mills themselves," Mr. Harrison said. "And to local residents who present their tax bills, we will provide this service for free."

Meanwhile, nearly one hundred and thirty residents have been provided jobs with the creation of the Hampton Light and Power Company. There are wheelwrights, sailmakers, mechanics, stone-sharpeners, and a whole construction crew which keeps the wooden mills in tip top shape.

The company does not make a profit as yet, but when it does, it will be shared among the stockholders who are, in fact, the customers.

"This is a dream come true," Mr. Harrison said.

And indeed it is.

If other municipalities are interested in learning more about Hampton Light and Power, they should write WIND, care of Dan's Papers, Main Street, Bridgehampton, N.Y. 11932. Private citizens who would like to purchase Hampton Light and Power T-shirts should send $5 to the same address.

Moondog

For thirty years, Moondog stood on the corner of 54th Street and Sixth Avenue. He was a majestic figure, well over six feet tall, and he stood there almost every day through rain, sleet and snow, selling his poems and sheet music and playing songs of his own making on instruments of his own design.

Those of us who saw Moondog will never forget him. He was as much a figure of New York City as the Empire State Building or the Statue of Liberty. Wearing robes and boots, a Viking helmet and a cape, he bore in one hand a seven foot spear and in the other a satchel of his music. Blind, he stared straight ahead at the middle distance, giving the impression of great dignity and total inaccessibility.

But Moondog was everything but inaccessible. From his stand on the corner of Sixth Avenue he was patient and kind to everyone who had the courage to meet him. And, over the years, he met children, office workers, housewives, businessmen and other musicians. Some of these other musicians — New York Philharmonic conductor Artur Rodzinski for one — thought very highly of his work and made repeated attempts to feed and shelter him and change his unorthodox lifestyle. But Moondog always politely refused every offer. He needed his freedom, he said, and as he approached old age, it was apparent to most that he would continue as he had always done, sleeping on the streets of the city, and living by the kindness of the people who came to see him at the corner of 54th Street and Sixth Avenue.

But today, Moondog is not at his regular corner,

and, in fact, he has not been seen in the city for the past several years. Many people have wondered whatever became of this landmark figure and just assumed that he met some tragic end to his unorthodox existence.

This, it turned out, is not the case at all. The fact is that Moondog has met a girl. And he has been swept off his feet just as clearly as any princess has ever been swept off her feet by a knight on a white horse.

Her name is Ilona Goebel, she is 27 years old, and she is small, slight, blond, and a resident of the village of Oer-Erkenschwick, West Germany. At the present time, Moondog, without his cape, helmet and spear is living with her and her family in the Goebel home halfway around the world.

Ilona Goebel met Moondog entirely by chance. At the time, Moondog was on what he thought would be a brief tour of Germany under the sponsorship of New York organist Paul Jordan. Jordan had thought that perhaps he could shake Moondog's lifestyle by some sort of tour, and so he offered to take Moondog to Europe, pay all his expenses, and play his music in concert in the capitals of Europe. It was an offer so great and so remarkable that Moondog, standing at the corner of 54th Street and Sixth Avenue, simply couldn't refuse.

Thus it was that Moondog was standing, in full battle regalia, on a street corner in Recklinghausen, West Germany. He was on his concert tour, certainly, but he was between his concerts with Paul Jordan, and so he was resuming his regular lifestyle, standing on the street corner, selling and giving away his poems and music.

Miss Goebel, a geology student, was walking down the street with her ten-year-old brother when she saw him. She came up and began a conversation.

There was nothing in the slightest unusual about this from either point of view. Ilona was enamored of the presence of Moondog, as many women have been in the past, and Moondog for his part was gentle and patient with the young woman and her brother as he always was. He had been doing this for over thirty years after all.

When Ilona Goebel left Moondog after her brief encounter, however, she spoke about him to her ten-year-old brother and asked how she liked him.

"I feel sorry for him," her brother said. "It must be cold on that street corner all day. And he doesn't seem to have any friends. Let's invite him home with us. Christmas is coming and he should have a home."

Ilona of course did not act on this suggestion at this time. Moondog was, after all, a bizarre figure in the town, and certainly she did not feel comfortable enough to invite him to her home.

But later on, when Ilona heard Moondog's music, she changed her mind. The music was so beautiful, she thought, and so original. It was impossible that a man could write music like that and live as he did.

Thus, Ilona Goebel returned to Moondog and stated her case. Moondog, she said, should give up living on the streets and should move in with her and her family in Oer-Erkenschwick.

Moondog, of course, refused.

The next day, however, Ilona was back. She would not give up, she told Moondog, and she insisted that he change his mind.

"What has it gotten you, standing on the corner in the same old way for thirty years?" she asked. "You keep trying and nothing keeps happening. Try something new."

And so, amazingly, Moondog agreed to go live with Ilona.

"She's sort of adopted me," Moondog told Paul

Jordan when he learned what was happening. "I feel at home here with Ilona and I feel at home here in Germany. So many great composers have lived and worked here. I want to work here too."

And so Moondog took off his helmet, set aside his cape and spear, and went with Ilona on the train to Oer-Erkenschwick, where he lives and composes today.

Moondog works on his music, and Ilona promotes it for him. She has given up her studies as a geologist and, as publisher, agent, producer and transcriber for him, has caused two records of his works to appear. One of these, on the Heritage label, is available in New York, and there are plans for two more albums before the end of the year. And then French State Radio, led by a young music critic named Martin Meissonier, even brought Moondog to Paris where he was able to conduct and perform his own work in concert.

In addition, Ilona has founded a sheet music publishing company for Moondog's work. She has called it the Managram Company, and she has made available on a worldwide basis the compositions that Moondog has produced.

Moondog, for his part, has given up everything but his long white beard and hair. Dressing now in regular trousers and shirts, he has also reverted to his original name of Louis Hardin. At 62 years of age, he is not all that distinguishable from other Americans living in West Germany.

"I am living in a composer's paradise," he recently told an American visitor at his new home. "I am surrounded by musicians, I get my meals on time. I'm warm, and most of all I'm free for my music."

Ilona smiled as Louis Hardin spoke to the visitor. "Louis and his music consume my life," she said simply.

I Name Thee...Oh...
Shinnecock Hills

It's amazing how people get worked up about place names. Out in Hollywood, former bandleader Rudy Vallee has gotten himself so excited about the name of the street he lives on, that he's decided to run for the city council. Mr. Vallee, it seems, lives on a small street in Hollywood with a name like Ridgewood Road or something, and about five years ago, he got it into his head the road should be really named Rue de Vallee in honor of himself. Mr. Vallee, was, after all, moderately famous, and names of other streets, particularly in Hollywood, have been changed to indicate that such-and-so lives on the street.

In any case, Mr. Vallee made his recommendation to the city councilmen, and the councilmen, after spending several years discussing the subject, finally decided to leave things as they were. This apparently has really infuriated Rudy Vallee, who, at the age of 72, is going to run for the council.

"(I'm going to) tear the guts out of some of the council members," he said, "and curb some of the arrogance and power of those little tin gods."

But if Mr. Vallee is having his problems with place names in California, it is as nothing compared to the problems the Parker Brothers are being faced with in Atlantic City, New Jersey. Parker Brothers, as you may know, is the well-to-do manufacturer of MONOPOLY, the wonderful game of make believe capitalism that has charmed millions of people since its development in 1935. It was back then, in the middle of the depression, the late Charles B. Darrow

220

of Philadelphia invented the game, choosing the streets and place names of Atlantic City, New Jersey. Mr. Darrow did this in honor of the fact that he had many pleasant summer vacations in Atlantic City.

Well, now the City Commission of Atlantic City is proposing to change the names of two of the famous streets in that town, specifically Mediterranean and Baltic Avenues. The commission is not planning to change the names because these streets were chosen by Mr. Darrow to be the cheapest properties on the monopoly board, but because the streets are actually just extensions of other streets, and the name just changes in the middle. This, according to Atlantic City Commissioner of Public Works, Arthur W. Ponzio, is very confusing.

Parker Brothers thinks differently. In fact, Edward P. Parker, the president of Parker Brothers, wrote a very strongly-worded protest to Commissioner Ponzio.

"Would you like to be the man to tell a Monopoly fanatic from California that the streets he came to see no longer exist?" he wrote, reminding the commissioner that Monopoly was doing a great deal more for Atlantic City than Atlantic City was doing for Monopoly. "Baltic and Mediterranean Avenues are not just local street names," Mr. Parker continued, with the violins rising in the background, "they must be included in the category containing such thoroughfares as Broadway, Trafalgar Square and the Champs-Elysees. Who would ever suggest changing their names? Baltic and Mediterranean Avenues belong to America."

Under this written assault, Mr. Ponzio seems to have been relatively unmoved. Although he was "certainly cognizant of the publicity" Atlantic City had received from the game, he said he was still planning to go ahead and change the two names.

Incidentally, as a result of his letter, several newspapers went and visited Edward Parker to get him to elaborate on the situation. One of the reporters pointed out that due to an oversight on the part of Mr. Darrow when he invented the game, the Atlantic City street Marven Gardens was accidentally misspelled Marvin Gardens. If the Atlantic City Commissioner agreed to keep from changing Baltic and Mediteranean Avenues, would Parker Brothers revise their Monopoly and change "Marvin Gardens" to Marven Gardens.

"We do not intend to change the spelling of the Monopoly property 'Marvin Gardens'," Mr. Parker said. "Perhaps the real Marven Gardens should consider changing its spelling."

Mr. Parker certainly is in no mood to compromise.

Eastern Long Island has had its share of name changes by the way. Early on, the village of Maidstone changed its name to Easthampton and nobody seemed to mind. When the railroad came in the mid-eighteenth century, it separated Easthampton into two words, East Hampton, and again nobody seemed to mind. South Hampton, meanwhile, suffered the reverse fate on behalf of the railroad and became Southampton, again without anyone objecting. Also, about 1900, the village of Good Ground became Hampton Bays without fanfare. It was only in 1905, when the village of Shinnecock Hills tried to change its name that people got all worked up. At the time, it was becoming fashionable to live in the "Hamptons," and so, the 200 people who lived in Shinnecock Hills, all of whom were summer residents, wrote up a petition to change the name of the village to

"Hampton Hills". They presented this petition to Southampton Township, only to be told it was invalid.

"This petition must be signed by the majority of the YEAR AROUND residents in Shinnecock Hills," the Town Supervisor told the summer people at the time.

"But there ARE no year-round people in Shinnecock Hills!" the petitioners replied. "We all go back to the City in the winter!"

It was then realized, however, there WAS one year-round resident of Shinnecock Hills, and that was the postmaster, Mr. Terwillger. He lived above the post office and forwarded everyone's mail all winter long.

The petitioners then went up to see Mr. Terwilliger and with great agitation explained what it was they wanted to do, and it all depended on him. Mr. Terwilliger rocked back and forth in his rocking chair for a minute, puffed on his pipe, and then rendered his decision.

"Nope," he said.

And it is still Shinnecock Hills today.

House on the Rampage

As you've probably noticed, the Coast Guard runs on a particularly tight budget. While the Army and the Navy and the Air Force get cost overruns and billions of dollars here and billions of there, the Coast Guard just manages to scrape by. Nobody knows exactly the reason for this, but whatever it is, it has always been that way.

For example, in the mid-nineteen fifties, when the Coast Guard abandoned their big lifesaving station on the Napeague between Amagansett and Montauk, they made provisions to move the big old building to Montauk, where they planned to put it on new foundations on Star Island for their new headquarters. Surely, the Army or Navy would have put out bids for the destruction of the old building, then put out more bids for the construction of the new buiding on Star Island, but then that was not, and is not the way the Coast Guard worked.

The big, three-story building was brought to Star Island in two stages. In the first stage, a house mover put the building up on skids and towed it in a northerly direction, across the dunes, across Montauk Highway and the railroad tracks, and finally to a small arc of a beach on the bay where it would be transferred to a raft and then towed through Long Island Sound to Montauk Harbor ten miles distant. The man who won the bid to tow this big building to Montauk was Carl Darenberg, the present owner of the Montauk Marine Basin. Carl was about twenty-eight at the time and had what he thought was a powerful boat. As things turned out, however, the towing of this building was a terrifying experience.

Carl waited for a very calm day to make his move. With a good weather forecast and good prospects, he took his boat and, together with a mate, went down to get the house. He had little difficulty in hooking up his lines to the raft. The raft, with the huge house on top, came off the beach quite easily, too. But once out to sea, with the journey just half over, the wind began to come up. At first, the wind seemed to be a good thing to the two men in the small inboard. It was a tailwind, and as it pushed the house from the rear, it seemed to take some of the strain off the small engine in Carl's boat two hundred feet in front.

After about fifteen minutes of this tailwind, however, the breeze seemed to stiffen, and the mate noticed a very strange thing.

"Better open the throttle," he said. "I think the house is gaining on us."

Sure enough, with the strong tailwind, the raft and the house were churning along at a remarkable speed. The towlines were slack, and were beginning to coil up.

But Carl Darenberg discovered a very interesting thing when he went to open up the throttle. It was already wide open as far as it would go. In fact, as things now stood, if the wind stayed up, as it seemed to have every indication of doing, the house would shortly catch up to them and pass them right out to sea.

The wind slackened a little bit, and Carl was able to race the house almost dead even for several miles. But then, when the wind picked up again, the house increased its momentum and gave every appearance of running right over them, if they didn't get out of the way. Less than fifty feet separated the house and the boat as the pair struggled on up to the entrance to Montauk Harbor and then right past it. A few fishermen on the jetty at the entrance to the Harbor stood staring with their mouths open.

"I've got an idea," Carl shouted.

"It better be a good one," the mate yelped.

Carl cut his engine and turned his rudder, steering clear of the house as it pulled alongside. Then, as the house and the boat were dead even, Carl leaped across to the raft. The mate, guessing what Carl was about, gunned the engine of the boat to keep abreast.

Carl tried the front door.

"It's locked," he shouted.

"Try around back," the mate replied.

Carl ran around the house, his feet thumping on the wooden planking of the raft, and found the back door was, indeed, unlocked. He disappeared inside, and then in a few moments, reappeared at a window on the second floor, and another and another. Soon ever window on that floor was open, and Carl had raced up to the third. Within five minutes, Carl had opened each of the thirty-two windows of that building, allowing the wind to go harmlessly in one side of the building and out the other. In a very short time, the house and the raft slowed down and came to a halt. The mate pulled the boat up, Carl leaped back aboard and proceeded to tow the house the

ROUTE OF THE MONTAUK COAST GUARD STATION

rest of the way home.

Carl's office today is just a few hundred yards from the main building of the Star Island Coast Guard Station. Every day he can look at that three-story white structure and reflect on the fact that if that back door had not been unlocked...well, maybe he'd just better not think about it.

Fun in IGA Parking Lot

A Mercedes SL 150 pulled up to the Bridgehampton IGA the other morning. This is a small convertible sports car, very expensive, and very elegant. This one was powder blue.

The car stopped in the parking lot there, and a man in a leather coat got out bearing a shopping list. He was quickly followed by the only other occupant of the car: a white, full-size poodle that seemed very enthusiastic and anxious to please.

"Get back in the car," the man said. And the poodle obediently climbed back in. The man closed the door, turned, and the poodle jumped right out over the door. It was a convertible after all.

"I thought I told you to stay," the man said, motioning the dog back in. They went through the same procedure, and again the dog wound up back on the parking lot pavement, wagging his tail, awaiting further instructions.

"Okay," the man said. "DON'T stay in the car. Sit."

The dog sat.

"And stay."

And the dog stayed. The man walked the twenty feet or so toward the supermarket, looked back once to see if the dog was staying, which he was, and then went inside.

The dog stayed where he was, sitting obediently alongside the blue Mercedes for a few minutes, and he awaited further instructions. But after a little while, as there were none forthcoming, and as he was an enthusiastic dog, and he was getting a little anxious, he stood up and went over to the IGA to get a better look.

I think his intent was just to go over to the window and sit down so he could look inside, but that is not what happened.

By chance, he walked onto the rubber mat just outside the sliding glass doors. Instantly, the mechanism that activates the doors began to hum. And the doors slid open.

I could have sworn I saw that poodle smile. He cocked his head gaily to one side, wagged his tail and trotted in.

Some Days It Doesn't Pay to Get Up

About two weeks ago, Alex Benkoczy decided to invite his grown son, and some of his son's friends, out for a fishing trip on his boat.

"Why don't you ask your boss," Alex said. "Maybe he'd like to go."

Shortly Michael Benkoczy called back his father in Sag Harbor. His boss, who was a Nassau County District Attorney investigator, would love to go. Also, what about the boss' brother? Alex said that would be fine, and so the plans were made to go out for a weekend of shark fishing Friday, Saturday and Sunday, September 22 to 24.

It was an elaborate trip. But it looked like fun. Around 3 o'clock on Thursday, Alex Benkoczy left his home on Main Street, Sag Harbor, and went over to the dock where he keeps his 42-foot yawl. He welcomed on board his mate, loaded the sailboat up with provisions and headed on out. He would sail leisurely through calm waters out to Montauk Harbor where he would meet his son and their guests at Captain's Marina. They would stay the night and then, the following morning, leave Captain's Marina early for the weekend at sea.

Out at Montauk, Alex Benkoczy met his son's boss, Joe Quinn. He also met Joe's brother John, who is the head of the New York State Lottery. Also, there was another guest, a mutual friend named James Nolan from Queens. There was a nice dinner, early to bed, and then a predawn departure. Captain Alex chugged out of Montauk Harbor using his auxiliary engine. Once out, he set his sails.

What you have read above seems like the beginning of a nice pleasant weekend of shark fishing. But, in fact, it was the beginning of one of the most bizarre weekends this group of six men or any six men have ever spent.

The trouble began around eleven o'clock that Friday night. They were twenty-five or thirty miles southeast of Block Island at that point, and they had been fishing all day without any luck. But then, the weather made a turn for the worse. And suddenly, the men found themselves pitching through twenty and thirty-foot seas. Some of the fishermen had gone to sleep. And some were still up. Alex talked about the situation, and it was decided to pull up the lines and try to ride the storm out. Radio contact was made with a passing vessel, and Alex indicated the trouble he was in. The passing vessel, which was a tugboat hauling an oil rig called "Platform to Victory," indicated she too was having trouble riding out the waves. The captains of the two ships decided to keep in constant contact by radio, but maintain five miles between themselves in order to avoid a possible collision.

Saturday morning, they reached a landfall. Much to their disappointment, they found they were off the twin radio towers of Napeague between Montauk and Amagansett. They had hoped they would come in to the east of Montauk Point so they could tuck into the safety of Gardiner's Bay. But they had overshot the mark, and there was no turning back. The wind would push them westerly, away from the Montauk Lighthouse, and in the direction of New York City. They would have to stay in the tremendous seas of the Atlantic, and take their luck there.

231

Most of the men had become seasick by this time, but sometime about three p.m. Saturday afternoon, Joe Quinn developed chest pains. Alarmed, everyone expressed fear that perhaps Joe was having a heart attack. Joe Quinn is 52.

At this point, therefore, Alex Benkoczy radioed his alarm to the United States Coast Guard at Shinnecock. They radioed back and asked for Joe's pulse rate and vital signs. When these were given, the Coast Guard decided Joe should be receiving medical attention. So they called Floyd Bennett Field with the hopes that a helicopter could be dispatched to effect a sea to air rescue.

Floyd Bennett, however, could not go out in the terrible weather, and so the Coast Guard then decided to send a rescue boat out to tow in the yawl.

"Where are you?" the Coast Guard asked.

"We can't see a damn thing," Alex replied. "Also, we've lost our rudder."

About six o'clock, however, Alex got a fix on the radio towers at Westhampton Beach. He was slowly being blown in the direction of New York. The Coast Guard would have to hurry if they wanted to fetch him.

Finally, about seven, the 44-foot Coast Guard Vessel "O-8" reached the sailboat. A line was shot across the bow, and eventually a tow line hooked up. Under great strain, the Coast Guard ship slowly began to make its way over towards the Shinnecock Inlet. Once inside, in the calm waters of the Bay, all would be fine.

One half mile from shore, however, a tow line from the Coast Guard ship fouled on its own propellor. The engine balked, then seized. And suddenly, there were two ships in serious trouble instead of one.

Quickly, the tow line between the two ships was cut. And the Coast Guard vessel drifted quickly in through the surf to a beached landing on the sand west of the Inlet. Alex put up some sails, and through the storm he could have jockeyed his yawl back out to sea. However, it seemed more important at this time to save his passenger rather than his ship.

"We are going to deliberately beach our sailboat," he radioed to the Coast Guard. "Have an ambulance ready to take Mr. Quinn off at the beach."

On shore, alarms were sounded, and the Aldrich Hand American Legion Rescue Squad in Hampton Bays raced into action. Driving through the storm, they arrived down at the beach where the two ships were now beached broadside. And carefully, with much risk to their own lives, they took Joe Quinn off the sailboat in a stretcher and carried him the 500 yards back up the sand, through the dunes to the waiting ambulance. The other men aboard both the Coast Guard ship and the sailboat leaped overboard and swam ashore through the darkness to waiting rescue cars. It was now midnight between Saturday night and Sunday morning.

*   *   *

Alex and the other men all went home to Sag Harbor. It had been a rough weekend, but it seemed to be all over now. Joe Quinn, who had been taken to the hospital, was found to be not so ill after all. His heart was fine. And his chest pains were just from dehydration and from muscle strain from throwing up a lot. He would probably be released in the morning.

But you know, there is an old story about the man who climbs Mount Everest, braves a typhoon, survives a landslide and an earthquake, and then breaks a leg slipping on a banana peel. And that old story is what proceeded to happen in real life to Captain Alex Benkoczy, the hero of this piece.

On Sunday morning, in the peace and quiet of Main Street, Sag Harbor, Alex Benkoczy began to hear stories about the coverage of the rescue by the local radio station. The newscaster there, Joe Ricker, had been issuing bulletins every hour or so.

"I thought I heard there was a dead man on board," someone said.

"Did I hear on the radio that you were shipwrecked on Shelter Island?"

Alex called up the radio station, WLNG, and asked if he could set the record straight.

"Send a man over with a tape recorder," Alex said. "I'll give you my account the way it really happened."

"I'm the only one here," Joe Ricker said. "It's Sunday. I can't leave the station. But if you'll come over here, I'll tape you at the station. And we'll get it on the midday news."

And so Alex went.

At the radio station, he was met at the door by Joe Ricker and ushered into a recording studio.

"Here, I'll just turn this tape on," Joe said. And then Joe Ricker stood up, turned, and bumped against a shelf that was holding up forty-one long playing records. The shelf came down, hit Alex in the head, and scattered records all over the place.

"It was like I got hit by lightning," Alex later said. "I don't remember a thing."

In fact, he was knocked cold, and the next thing he remembers is a doctor peering into his eyes on a hospital bed in Southampton. Perhaps five hours had passed.

Alex is back home now. He spent almost two weeks in the hospital recovering from the knock on the head, which was diagnosed as a concussion. They tell him his back will continue to be sore for perhaps another month.

And, ironically, Alex's 42-foot yawl is now in drydock at Bob Schwenck's Ship Ashore Marina, directly across the street from the radio station where Alex got his knock on the head.

"They sent a big Coast Guard cutter out from Montauk to rescue the two beached boats," Alex told me. "But then that broke down and had to anchor. So they sent another. Eventually, they got everything off and towed into Shinnecock. My boat is a little banged up, but it will be all right. And I'm a little banged up. But I'll be all right, too."

Naked Came The Potato Farmer

A report has appeared in NEWSDAY that a Bridgehampton farmer was seen riding his tractor in the nude. According to NEWSDAY, someone telephoned the Southampton Village Police to report the shocking occurrence, and was told that although Bridgehampton was not under the jurisdiction of the Village police, the complaint would be forwarded to the proper authorities. The article went on to say that the Village police phoned the Town police, and an entry was made on the police blotter to the effect that perhaps the farmer "has found a new way to raise potatoes."

Everyone knows that NEWSDAY is running these articles about the East End in order to try to boost it's circulation in the area. Dan's Papers believes the nude tractor report was a put-up job, and the man riding around in the buff was nothing more than a NEWSDAY lackey, trying to create some news. How do we know this? Well, the field where farmer Charlie Vanderveer plows in the nude is completely obstructed from the road. It would have been impossible for anyone to have seen him and his tractor there, much less report it.

Diary of The Walking Dunes

Charlie Stuart walked out the door of P.S. 138 and walked down Eighth Avenue to 53rd Street. It was one of the hottest June days he could remember and, in the heat, the sidewalk shimmered off into the distance. He walked past the pizza place, past the record store, and past the Gristedes, shifting his schoolbooks from one arm to the other. Jeez, it was hot.

Finally, he arrived at the shade of the large awning of his apartment house. The doorman opened the glass for him, and he was shortly in the relative coolness of apartment 2133. His mother was in the kitchen, in the hot kitchen, working over something hot on the stove. His father, his uniform and his gun draped over a chair, was sitting by the only air conditioner in the house, watching the Mets on TV.

"What 'cha cooking?" Charlie asked, as he set his books down on the kitchen table.

"I'm baking some bread," his mother said. "Have you got a lot of homework?"

"Yeah. You know it's a pain. It's a real pain, when you've already been accepted at college to still have to do your homework."

Charlie's mother smiled and bent over to open the oven door. The smell of hot fresh bread wonderously filled the hot dank room. Charlie picked up his books and headed for his room. It was too hot to play stickball. Instead, he'd see who he could raise on the air waves. He sat down on his metal chair, surveyed the vast array of metal tubes and dials on the table in front of him, then flicked on the power.

"This is W2AJAK, W2AJAK," he said into his microphone. "Anyone there?" There was a crackling sound over the loudspeaker, but no reply.

I guess I'm the only guy operating a ham set in this heat, Charlie thought. He changed the channel and tried again.

"This is W2AJAK, W2AJAK," he said. "Come in. This is a CQ, CQ, CQ. Anyone around?"

Still there was silence. One of Charlie's math books, at that moment, slid to the floor and Charlie bent over to pick it up. Suddenly there was a voice on the line.

"This is W2AXXI. Come in W2AJAK."

The voice was loud and clear. It sounded as if it were coming from a set down the hall.

"Hello there! Where are you? This is W2AJAK, Charlie Stuart, on West 56th Street in Manhattan. Where are you?"

"I'm out in Montauk," the voice said. "I just got this thing working. I'm up on a sand dune."

"Who are you W2AXXI?"

"Harrison's the name. Beachcombing's my game.

I'm up on top of a sand dune, and I've built me a little wooden shelter. I've got to keep this little ham set out of the wind. It's blowing quite a bit here. Got to keep sand from getting into the wires.''

"Wow!" said Charlie. "You know what it's like here in Manhattan? It's maybe a hundred degrees. You sure are lucky if getting sand in your set is your only problem.''

Some interference suddenly came on the line. A loud buzzing sound, maybe a power saw or something. And when it went away, the man named Harrison was gone. Nothing Charlie was able to do would bring him back.

At dinner that night, Charlie excitedly told his parents how he had reached a beachcomber on a sand dune in Montauk. Nobody seemed particularly interested in it.

"That's nice," his mother said.

*   *   *

The next day, the second straight day of the heat wave, Charlie tried to raise the beachcomber again. He worked at it for half an hour without success and was just about to give up when the voice came on again.

"Mr. Harrison!"

"Just Harrison to you.''

"Where were you? What happened to you yesterday?''

"I thought you had gone. So I went. I've been out gathering wood. I'm making a pretty good shack here.''

"What's it like out there?''

"Oh, it's quite nice. Sort of cool and windy, and very quiet. That's the main thing. Very quiet. There's not a soul for miles around. I can just lie here and enjoy myself.''

239

"Do you have a bathing suit?"

"Oh, I've got lots of stuff. I've got a suitcase full. And a whole lot of paperback books, too. I'm going to be here a while."

"You are?"

"I'm making a study of this place. It's called the Walking Dunes. So they say. They tell me the wind blows these sand dunes around, and if you watch them closely, you can actually see them move."

"You can?"

"So they say. I'm gonna live in this little shack I've built, and I'm going to keep some notes. There's a dune about forty feet high about forty feet away from here. We'll see what it does."

"That sounds exciting."

"Boring is more like it. But it's something to do. At the end of the summer, I'll put all my notes together and write a book about it. Probably sell it, and make enough money to go spend the winter somewhere."

"Gee. Can I talk to you?"

"You're talking to me now."

"I mean on a regular basis. Could we talk every day on this channel? You could tell me how you're making out."

"If you want."

"Okay. Every day at three thirty, this channel. I'll be here."

And that was the last Charlie Stuart was able to say to Harrison. The transmitting hum was gone, and the line was suddenly clear. Harrison was gone.

*   *   *

All through his classes the next day, through algebra, through geology and through chemistry, Charlie Stuart wondered about this man named Harrison. What kind of a person was he? What sort of man would just go out and camp on a sand dune? When the bell rang ending classes for the day, Charlie hurried home and without a single word to his parents, hurried to his room to flick on his ham set.

"How are you doing?" Charlie asked after he had made contact. It was a fairly stupid question, considering all the questions boiling around in his mind.

"Well, you know how it is," Harrison said in his gravelly voice. "Sometimes you win, sometimes you lose."

"Tell me, what do you look like?"

"Look like? Oh, I don't know. Not too tall, not too short."

"Do you have a beard?"

"Yes, I have a beard."

241

"A big bushy beard?"

"A big, bushy beard. It's turnin' grey, though."

"What else?"

"Ask me something else. Ask me about the shack I've been building."

"How's your shack?"

"Shack's done. It's got a window and a door. I found a door. I thatched the roof. It's a good, sturdy little shack. I can even lie down in it, and my feet don't stick out. I put a calendar up on the wall."

"A PLAYBOY calendar?"

"An Amagansett Lumber and Coal Company Calendar. It's got a picture of a covered bridge on it. Things like that."

"Have you got covered bridges out there?"

"No. I don't think there are even any bridges. It's just a standard calendar you get by sending away. What date is today?"

"The fifteenth."

"Ahah. I was off by a day. How about that. Thought it was the fourteenth. Hmmm."

There was a long pause. Charlie, with all the things that had been going through his mind, couldn't think of anything else to ask him.

"Well," said Harrison. "Got to be going. Lots of things to do here. Tomorrow, get yourself a tape recorder. We'll do some taping."

"Hey!" Charlie shouted. But it was too late. Harrison was gone.

*   *   *

The next afternoon, Charlie Stuart left school, walked down 53rd Street and stopped at the JLH Audio Center between Eighth and Ninth Avenue. He had with him forty-two dollars, which were his life savings.

"Does it have to be anything special?" Angie the

242

Greek wanted to know. Angie was Charlie's friend, a high school drop out, who was wearing the suit and tie he always wore at the store.

"I don't know, Angie. I'm just doing some taping off of my ham set."

"Well, then you won't need anything special. What are you taping off of your ham set?"

A half an hour later, Charlie and Angie the Greek were in Apartment 2133 trying to raise Harrison out on the sand dune.

"W2AJAK, W2AJAK, calling Montauk. Come in Montauk."

"Maybe he's not there," said Angie the Greek.

"He's there. I know he's there."

"Hello, this is W2AXXI," crackled a voice over the loudspeaker. "Have you got that tape recorder?"

"Yes, I have."

"Turn it on then. Here we go. This will be tape number one, June seventeenth. The Diary of the Walking Dunes by Samuel Harrison."

"Wow," said Angie the Greek.

"It's been a peaceful day in the walking dunes. The temperature is seventy-three degrees, and it is now three-thirty two in the afternoon. I have completed measurements to three walking dunes for the day, and since I have been here for three days, I can make comparative studies. Walking Dune One, which is to the south of me, measured fifty-eight feet away when I first got here. It is now fifty-one feet from the eastern edge of my cabin. A movement of seven feet. Walking Dune Two is to the east of me. It measured seventy-one feet from this cabin three days ago, and today measures seventy feet, a movement of one foot. Walking Dune Three is to the north and was forty-two feet away three days ago, while today it is down to thirty-nine feet. The wind is from the southwest, and has been for a couple of days. A young couple came up here yesterday. They parked on Sand Dune Number Three and had a picnic. They might have seen me, I don't know. Anyway, they didn't wave or anything, just ate their food and left. Sunset was obscured by a big cloud. The sky turned a pink, then an orange, then finally a deep maroon with long shafts of orange through the center of the sky. End of tape one.''

There was a buzzing sound, and then Harrison was gone.

"W2AXXI. W2AXXI. Harrison. Harrison?''

"I don't believe it,'' Angie the Greek said. "I just don't believe it.'' He took out a comb and ran it through his hair, then smoothed it with his hand. "Fantastic.''

* * *

The days turned into weeks, and June turned into July. Every afternoon, Charlie and Angie the Greek would sit up in Charlie's bedroom and tape record Harrison's Walking Dunes Diary. But something odd was happening that Charlie and Angie the Greek were only beginning to realize. Here, for example, is the diary entry for the first day of July.

"Tape number fourteen, July one. The Diary of the

Walking Dunes by Samuel Harrison. I've been fishing over by a small pond I found up near Long Island Sound. Caught two flounder there. The water is clear as glass, and you can see right to the bottom of the pond, which must be seven or eight feet deep. I'm cleaning the fish and will have them tonight. Also, took in two jugs of drinking water from the pond. No way to test them, so I'll boil them up before I drink them. Looks pure enough to me, though. Dune One is now twenty-two feet away to the south. Seems to be a little taller, too. Dune Two is twenty-seven feet to the east. Dune three is eighteen feet to the west. I'm a little sleepy, got a little sunstroke, so I'll be signing off for the day. See you tomorrow."

Again came the familiar buzzing sound. Charlie and Angie sat there in silence thinking about this tape. Neither of them had to tell the other what was on their mind. The dunes had moved considerably closer. One had even seemed to grow taller, or so Harrison said. Charlie packed up the tape in the case next to the others, and the two boys left the bedroom and headed out toward the elevator.

"Don't forget to be home by six," Charlie's mother said as he passed through the kitchen.

* * *

At three-thirty, Charlie flipped the switch turning on the set and turned the dial to the frequency for Harrison. Angie opened the tape box and took out the next tape.

"W2AJAK, W2AJAK calling Montauk. Come in W2AXXI."

"This is W2AXXI. Howdy do. Tape number forty-one, July twenty-eight. The Diary of the Walking Dunes by Samuel Harrison. The temperature is seventy-eight degrees. I had a little trouble

245

getting that temperature reading this afternoon. The thermometer is tacked up on the north wall of the cabin on the outside. Sometime this morning Dune Three started climbing the wall, and apparently covered it up. I went out at noon and dug it out, and tacked it further up the wall. It should be okay for the rest of the day anyway. The way in and out of this place, by the way, is through the window only. The door on the south side has been completely covered up by Dune One now. No way I can get it clear. Just hope it holds. Measurements to all three dunes are now almost zero. I still measure from the edge of the cabin to the middle of the dune as near as I can determine. Dune one is now eight feet away. Dune two is nine feet and Dune three is seven feet. Wind is from the southwest. Food stores are pretty good. I'm only half way through the creamed corn, and I've only today had to start opening the baked beans. Heaven knows how I'll get any more."

"What do you think?" Angie asked.

"What?"

"You want to go out there? My car's running."

Charlie thought about this for a long time. He flipped off the master switch.

"Let's wait until tomorrow. What I'll do is, if things look bad, I'll cut in in the middle of his tape and ask him what he thinks. We can't do much more than that."

*   *   *

All the rest of the day and into the night, Charlie Stuart worried about Samuel Harrison. He ate very little of his dinner, and did none of his homework. The following day, he went to his classes mechanically, as if in a dream. He heard nothing of what was going on. And then, at 3:30 in the afternoon, he and Angie were up in his room, nervously trying to raise W2AXXI in Montauk.

"This is W2AXXI," the voice finally said much to their relief. "Harrison here. Let me tell you it's dark in here. Can hardly see what I'm doing anymore. Tape number forty-two, July twenty-nine. The Diary of the Walking Dunes by Samuel Harrison..."

"You want us to come out there?" Charlie cut in.

"Hey, who is that?"

"It's me, Charlie. You want us to drive out to Montauk? We could come get you. Help dig you out."

"Is all this being put down on the tape?"

"Yes, it is."

"Well, hell, you're ruining the diary. I've got to do the diary. This is the most important entry of all of them."

"Oh."

"Okay now, stay off the line. I'll start again. This is tape number forty-two, July twenty-nine. The Diary of the Walking Dunes by Samuel Harrison. I've been up half the night working on these graphs and charts. Near as I can figure, the three walking dunes I've been plotting show a distinct pattern. When the wind is blowing in one direction, they move about six, seven feet a day, depending upon the strength of the wind. When the wind blows in the opposite direction, however, they move only one foot, but it's STILL IN THE SAME DIRECTION. In other words, the dunes seem to be heading somewhere, and the wind only slows 'em down or speeds 'em up...Hold on a minute."

Charlie and Angie looked at each other anxiously.

"Had a little problem there," Harrison continued. "Roof started to make funny noises. Got the whole thing propped up with a big timber now. Where were we? Right. Even more interesting is the fact that each of the dunes is heading in a totally different direction from every other. Dune Number

One, for example, which was on my south, headed due north. It ran over a group of pine trees about twenty feet away that I was using for firewood at night. Buried 'em completely. It's now covered the door and is weighing heavy on the roof. Dune Number Two was on the east and headed west in the same way. And Dune Three up on the north just rolled right down due south about eight feet a day. I don't know exactly where all the dunes are this morning. Last measurement was taken yesterday, and you've got that one. But Dune Three is now up over the window, and I'm afraid to open it to find out how deep it is out there. If I didn't know better, the way these dunes have headed straight for this cabin, I might come to the conclusion that they..."

Over the loud speaker, there came a great cracking noise and a series of crashes. Both Charlie and Angie jumped up. There were more crashes, and then, nothing. Just the buzzing sound.

"Come on!" shouted Angie.

The two boys raced through the rest of the house, out into the hall and down the elevator. In the street, they ran down the avenue and off into a side street where Angie's Pontiac was parked. Jumping in, they

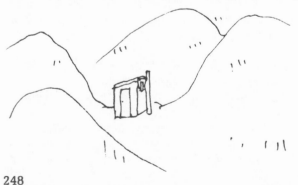

headed across town for the Mid-Town Tunnel. It seemed to take forever. But soon they were out on the Long Island Expressway, racing for Montauk. Neither boy said a word. They went through the small towns of the Hamptons, stopped at a gas station, got directions to the Walking Dunes, and in another twenty minutes were there.

The boys got out of their car, took off their shoes and raced barefoot into the dunes. The dunes were far larger than they imagined. They stretched for several miles along the arc of a bay, then several more miles along Long Island Sound.

"Over here," Angie shouted. "Look. That dune is enormous. It must be eighty feet high."

Surely, it was the biggest of the walking dunes. The boys ran toward it, then scaled it, climbing up to the very top.

"This has got to be the dune," Charlie said. "Look, there's the pond he was talking about. And over there, the tops of some covered up pine trees. This has got to be it."

The boys got down on their hands and knees and began to dig. It was a tremendous task. And no matter how far they dug, there was nothing. An

hour later, dusk was coming on, and they were exhausted. They rested against the side of the deep hole they had dug, nearly six feet deep. There was nothing more they could do.

"What's this?" Angie asked.

Sticking out of the side of the sand was a sheaf of paper. Angie pulled it out. It was paper clipped at the top and had the days of the week and the word AUGUST on it. On the top was written Amagansett Lumber and Coal Company. There was a large, beautiful color picture of a covered bridge.

COLD DUCK

ATTILA THE HEN

CHICKEN CROQUETTES

MOBY DUCK.

"AT THAT MOMENT LORENZO RUSHES ONSTAGE TO TELL ANTONIO HE IS COMPLETELY SURROUNDED. BUT ANTONIO WILL NOT SURRENDER. INSTEAD HE SINGS AN ARIA TO THE VIRGIN BEATRICE. AS THE CURTAIN FALLS, THE SHIP IS GOING UP IN FLAMES AND ANTONIO IS MAKING HIS WAY TO THE POOPDECK WHERE..."

254